Sort Out Your Family Finances

Bob Reeves

For UK order enquiries: please contact Bookpoint Ltd,
130 Milton Park, Abingdon, Oxon OX14 4SB.
Telephone: +44 (0) 1235 827720. Fax: +44 (0) 1235 400454.
Lines are open 09.00–17.00, Monday to Saturday, with a 24-hour
message answering service. Details about our titles and how to
order are available at www.teachyourself.com

Long renowned as the authoritative source for self-guided
learning – with more than 50 million copies sold worldwide –
the **Teach Yourself** series includes over 500 titles in the fields of
languages, crafts, hobbies, business, computing and education.

British Library Cataloguing in Publication Data: a catalogue record
for this title is available from the British Library.

This edition published 2010 by Hodder Education, part of
Hachette UK, 338 Euston Road, London NW1 3BH.

The **Teach Yourself** name is a registered trade mark of
Hodder Headline.

Copyright © 2010 Bob Reeves

Typeset by MPS Limited, A Macmillan Company.

Printed in Great Britain for Hodder Education, an Hachette UK
Company, 338 Euston Road, London NW1 3BH, by CPI Cox &
Wyman, Reading, Berkshire RG1 8EX.

The publisher has used its best endeavours to ensure that the
URLs for external websites referred to in this book are correct and
active at the time of going to press. However, the publisher and
the author have no responsibility for the websites and can make no
guarantee that a site will remain live or that the content will remain
relevant, decent or appropriate.

Hachette UK's policy is to use papers that are natural, renewable
and recyclable products and made from wood grown in sustainable
forests. The logging and manufacturing processes are expected to
conform to the environmental regulations of the country of origin.

Impression number   10 9 8 7 6 5 4 3 2 1
Year   2014 2013 2012 2011 2010

Front cover: © Digifoto Sapphire/Alamy

Back cover: © Jakub Semeniuk/iStockphoto.com, © Royalty-Free/Corbis,
© agencyby/iStockphoto.com, © Andy Cook/iStockphoto.com,
© Christopher Ewing/iStockphoto.com, © zebicho – Fotolia.com,
© Geoffrey Holman/iStockphoto.com, © Photodisc/Getty Images,
© James C. Pruitt/iStockphoto.com, © Mohamed Saber – Fotolia.com

Photo credits: p. xxviii: © PhotoAlto; p. 16: © Ingram Publishing
Limited; p. 32: © Stockbyte/Photolibrary Group Ltd; p. 50: © Corbis;
p. 66: © Ingram Publishing Limited; p. 84: © Ingram Publishing
Limited; p. 100: © Photodisc/Getty Images; p. 118: © PhotoAlto;
p. 140: © Ingram Publishing Limited; p. 160: © Stockdisc/Corbis;
p. 176: © Comstock Images/Photolibrary Group Ltd

Contents

Meet the author

Welcome and thanks for buying *Sort Out Your Family Finances*!

You have probably paid around a tenner for this book. If it does its job properly it will pay for itself if you follow any one of the tips and guidelines within its ten key chapters. Here are a few examples:

▶ Are you making the most of your and your children's tax-free savings allowances?
▶ Are you paying too much for insurance or even paying twice for the same cover?
▶ Are you regularly paying unnecessary bank charges and fees?
▶ Are you paying too much when you borrow money?
▶ Do you regularly over-spend at the end of each month and end up running on your overdraft?

When I discuss money or personal finance with friends and colleagues the same comments come up time and time again. First, it can be boring. Second, it can be complicated. Third, it changes so fast that it's impossible to keep up. There is an element of truth to all of these! With this in mind, in this book I have broken the large and complicated world of finance into ten manageable chunks and tried to explain each chunk in a succinct and non-technical way. I have also tried to give some common sense guidelines and rules of thumb along the way.

I have delved into my educational and working background in the financial services sector for much of it. I have also drawn upon my work for a finance education charity, developing personal finance training programmes that are being used by approximately 30,000 young people.

However, I have to say the most useful experience has been what I have learnt along the way from bringing up two children who I now consider to be 'grown up' but not quite independent. There is no substitute for real life.

About the author

Bob started his career in the financial services sector having completed a BA(Hons) in Business Studies. For many years he worked for one of the country's leading financial services companies mainly involved in training roles. This involved working within some of the UK's largest banks, building societies, retailers and insurers.

He later retrained as a teacher specializing in business and ICT. He has taught on a range of business and ICT courses over the years with students as young as four and as old as eighty. He has taught on specialized finance and accounts courses for the past 12 years covering various aspects of business and personal finance.

He has written several textbooks on ICT and business topics and more recently has been working with one of the country's leading finance education charities. This involves helping young people learn about the world of personal finance and getting them to consider their own attitudes and behaviour in relation to financial matters.

He has experienced most aspects of family finance first-hand being the father of two grown-up sons, both of whom took very different career routes. He has also run his own successful small business for the past five years.

Only got a minute?

Let's face it, many of us don't find dealing with our finances as exciting as some of the other things we do in life. Coupled with that, the world of money and personal finance appears complex and ever-changing. It is possible though to break the financial world down into manageable chunks and find plain explanations and common sense advice in dealing with the family finances. In doing this we will get a closer look at every stage of our financial lives, from cradle to grave.

If there is one thing that everyone should do on the personal finance front it is to create a budget plan. A budget plan lists all your income and spending. It helps you to identify areas of over-spending and shows you where you can make small economies that can add up to big savings.

Our children cost us a shocking amount of money from birth to age 18 and beyond. Starting right at the beginning you need to look at how to set up Child Trust Funds and other savings accounts. Finance plays a key part in every stage of your child's education, from childcare to school fees right into further and higher education. By planning for every stage you can ease the burden considerably.

Moving on to borrowing and saving, there are various ways in which you can borrow money and calculate how much this is costing you. You can also work out the best and cheapest methods of borrowing to achieve the lifestyle you want. On the flip side of the same coin are your savings and investments. There is a range of opportunities that are available to you both in the short and long term. Much depends on your attitude to risk and return. You also need to consider your pension as soon as you can.

Household expenses make up the biggest monthly expense and most of this is through the mortgage. There are many mortgage products on offer and many ways of reducing or curtailing the amount you pay. You can also carry out comparisons of other household expenses including the utility bills and examine whether it is worth switching to new suppliers. Shopping around for financial products and services and knowing how to choose the best and most appropriate deal can cut your costs.

Related to housing are the costs of buildings and contents insurance. In addition there is a whole range of insurance products out there covering everything from your car to your pets. Learn how to make judgements about insurance and how to reduce the premiums you might pay.

The world of banking has had a bit of a battering recently. Taking a look at the various accounts they have to offer, as well as looking at what you get from your bank and how much you are paying for it, can lead to a healthy saving on banking costs.

Learn how your income tax and National Insurance is calculated and check you are paying the right amount. Discover all the other taxes that eat into your income and check whether you are entitled to any benefits.

Few of us can live without debt so we need to look at the most beneficial ways of dealing with it. Part of this is to do with managing necessary debts. However, it is also about staying out of debt crisis and knowing what to do if you feel you are getting into trouble and making use of the help and support available.

5 Only got five minutes?

Budgeting

In many households it is quite common for expenses to be higher than income. This is because we want to buy more things than we can afford. Creating a budget will help you to keep track of your spending to stop this happening. People often don't realize how much they are spending and tend to underestimate the amount that they spend. Creating a budget will help you to work out the actual amount you spend.

How often have you said: 'I don't know where all my money goes'? Creating a budget plan helps you to break down all of your spending into categories so you can analyse exactly how much you are spending on different things. You might get a shock when you create your budget plan and find that you are spending too much money on some things or even paying for things you don't use.

Children and students

A recent survey estimated that the average cost of bringing up a child from birth to age 21 is around £180,000. The research also found that around £50,000 of this is on childcare and education, based on using the state education system. This total goes up significantly to around £250,000 if you send your offspring to private school. To put that into some kind of perspective, you will be spending around £8,500 per year on each of your children. That's around £23.50 a day, so only the price of a reasonably priced pub meal for two!

By looking at each of the key stages in children's lives from birth through to university you can, with planning, lessen the financial pressure of doing the best for your children. For example, you can look at the most beneficial ways of investing the Child Trust Fund that you are entitled to from the government. A careful examination of the costs of childcare and school fees can take you right up to the point where your youngsters leave home.

Borrowing money

On the surface, borrowing money seems to be a fairly simple transaction. You borrow the money from an organization, usually a bank or loan company and then you pay them back, plus interest. The repayments are usually made monthly and are calculated so that after a certain number of months, the debt is cleared.

The amount of interest you pay back is calculated as an Annual Percentage Rate (APR) and any company that lends money must by law publicize their APR prominently in their advertising and literature. In simple terms, if you borrow £1,000 for one year with an APR of 10% you will pay back £1,100, therefore paying £100 for the credit facility.

In reality it is more complex than this and looking carefully at the various methods of borrowing money will help you to consider the most appropriate type of borrowing for your situation.

Savings and investments

Saving money is the simple act of putting some money aside for later. Usually this involves putting the money somewhere safe where it will increase in value, usually by earning interest. Effectively your savings are 'investments' as you hope that the value of your savings pot will grow over time.

There are lots of reasons why people save money and, in common with other aspects of financial services, there are hundreds of options. There are a number of issues to consider: what you are saving for; how quickly you might need to get hold of your money; what impact this has on interest rates; how long you are prepared to invest your money; how much risk you are willing to take with your savings/investments.

You can learn how to look at the wide range of savings products available and consider the factors that lead to a higher return, including an analysis of risk.

Household expenses

For many households, the monthly mortgage payment represents the biggest single expense that they face. Add in other expenses directly related to owning and running a home, such as insurance, maintenance, utility bills and phone bills and many families will find well over half of their income disappearing before they even start spending money on things that are enjoyable.

By looking at mortgages in general and examining the different types of mortgage deals on the market you can make an informed choice on the one that best suits you. In addition, you can learn ways to manage other financial matters directly related to owning your own home including buildings and contents insurance, utility and phone bills.

Insurance

All insurance operates on the basic principle that the more risky something is, the higher the insurance premium. Often the decision you have to make is whether it is worth getting insurance at all; or you may simply be looking to reduce the amount of insurance premiums that you pay, while still covering yourself against major risks.

Your attitude to insurance is largely down to your attitude to risk. Some people only take out insurance where it is compulsory and don't bother with anything else. Other people prefer to cover themselves for all eventualities. You can pay home contents insurance for years and never make a claim. Alternatively you might have a bad year where you get burgled, crash your car and have all your luggage stolen on holiday. Life is unpredictable.

By looking at all the major types of insurance, you can decide whether it is worth taking out for your family. Each type is explained in clear terms in this book.

Banking

We need banks as they provide us with: somewhere safe to keep our money; convenient methods of paying for things; interest on our money. Banks need us as we provide them with: cash deposits that they can invest to make yet more money; interest payments on borrowing; payments for services.

The world of banking is very competitive with all the big banks vying for our custom. The range of bank accounts available can be daunting but it is possible to sift through the terminology to figure out which is most appropriate for your needs. You can also learn to easily grasp banks statements, the clearing system and bank charges.

Tax, National Insurance and benefits

This book analyses the 'tax burden' on each individual. This is the total amount of income tax, National Insurance and all the so-called 'hidden taxes' where we are paying tax and duties on other things. It is difficult to estimate how much we spend on taxes as part of our income. We do know that the average UK resident pays 20%

on their earnings and a further 11% in National Insurance. Add to that an estimated 17% of disposable income going on other taxes including council tax, VAT and petrol duties and you are losing about half your income.

Understanding the basics of how the tax and National Insurance systems work can lead to ways to reduce your personal tax burden and check if you have claimed for the full range of benefits that you might be entitled to.

Buying financial products and services

Most of us spend quite a lot of time shopping around for the best deal. The more expensive the product, the more time we tend to spend looking into the alternatives. We may go to several websites and shops to check what we can get for our money. In fact, the retail world knows we do this, which is why you find, for example, all the car showrooms or large DIY stores in the same part of town. They know that we want to carry out some 'comparison shopping' and so conveniently locate themselves next to their biggest rivals.

Most of us are quite good at comparison shopping and do it with cars, electrical items, computers, clothes, petrol and even food. However, we are not so good at doing it with financial products. This is probably because buying financial products is not as much fun. However, we stand to save large amounts of money if we can be bothered to do it.

It also helps to find out what advice is on offer and what consumer protection we have.

Dealing with debt

There is a tendency to think of all debts as a bad thing, but this is not necessarily the case. For example, very few of us could afford to buy our own houses without taking on an enormous debt in the form of a mortgage. There are other occasions in life when we choose to take on debts to get what we want now, and then manage the debt over the coming months and years.

Much of this comes down to your own personal attitude towards borrowing money. Some people steadfastly refuse to take on loans or credit cards, while others would never dream of saving up for something when they can get it now, even if it means paying extra for it in the long run.

There are two main aspects to debt. Debt management is when you have a plan to manage your debts. Debt crisis is when you can no longer afford to pay off your debts and are unable to make the basic monthly payments.

By knowing your options and the pitfalls you can avoid getting into debt crisis or, if the worst has already happened, understand more about how you may be able to get yourself out of it.

Introduction

This book covers everything you need to know about family finances from the 'cradle to the grave'. In it you will discover some scary statistics, like how much it costs to bring up a child, or how much money you need to save now to have a decent retirement. You will also learn about a massive range of financial products and services to help you decide whether or not they are for you. Along the way there is advice on how to budget effectively, where to keep your money, how to avoid paying too much for things you don't need, how to make the most out of your money and how to protect yourself for that 'rainy day'.

One of the problems when looking at the world of finance is that it can appear to be a bit boring. If we were in the market for a new car or a holiday we might get quite excited about shopping around for the best deal. When it comes to financial products that excitement factor often just isn't there. As a result we can end up ignoring financial matters or making snap decisions about what financial products and services to buy.

The world of finance can also sometimes appear to be complex, which gives the financial services providers a bit of a head-start on us. **Investments**, pensions and mortgages for example are all complex products and the people that sell them to us spend hours on training courses learning about them. But we have to make our decisions often based purely on advertising literature and whatever the salesperson tells us.

There are thousands of different financial products and services that you can buy and thousands of different providers. To make sense of all of this, this book has been broken down into ten main areas of finance:

▶ *budgeting*
▶ *children and students*

- ▶ *borrowing money*
- ▶ **savings** *and investments*
- ▶ *household expenses*
- ▶ **insurance**
- ▶ *banking*
- ▶ *tax and National Insurance and benefits*
- ▶ *buying financial products and services*
- ▶ *dealing with debt.*

Each chapter takes a different theme and explains all aspects of it. For example, the chapter on children and students looks at all aspects of finance from birth through to going to university. As the world of personal finance is so complex and there is so much small print, each chapter includes web links where you can read the finer detail on individual aspects.

The personal finance journey

Money plays an important part in all of our lives. Most of us will have key events in our life at which point finance and money are more important than others. You could look at this as a life cycle:

Childhood: we cost our parents a small fortune in everyday living expenses. They may set up **savings accounts** or investments for us. We get small lump sums of money, for example when it is our birthday, that we put into our first bank **account**. We go to school, which might be private, costing our parents a large fortune.

Teenage years: we learn to drive and want car insurance. We perhaps want to go on our first holiday without the parents. We get a part-time job. We can get **credit** for the first time at the age of 18.

Students: we go off to university, which will probably cost about £10,000 a year. We run up large debts that will have to be paid later.

We work part-time and perhaps have to start paying tax and **National Insurance**. We perhaps have a **gap year**. We have to manage our own finances for the first time and start to realize why our parents were so stressed all the time.

Early twenties: we want to leave home which means renting or trying to get on the housing ladder. We try to save enough for a **deposit** on a house. Money is tight as we are just starting out on our careers. We need to budget very carefully and shop around for the best deals. Our monthly outgoings are high.

Parenthood: perhaps we start a family of our own so now we are responsible for the small fortune that children cost. Our salary now has to cover an extra person. Perhaps one partner gives up work or goes part-time to look after the kids. We have to think about pensions. We may need a bigger house. We need to think about life insurance and providing an income should the worst happen.

Divorce: if we do have to go through this, it may mean selling the family home, dividing up the assets and perhaps starting again with a new mortgage. This may all have to be done on a single income.

Retirement: we want to stop work, cruise round the world and grow vegetables. We want to pay off our mortgage and buy an annuity with the money we have been saving into our **pension**. We start to think about what we might be able to leave our children.

Death: this can be a difficult aspect to contemplate but many financial decisions relate to it. We need our pensions to last as long as we do. We need to think about what we are leaving behind for our family. We may need insurance in case it happens while we still have dependants.

The financial services providers are well aware of this life-cycle too so they will be marketing their products and services to you at these key stages of your life. This book will take you through every stage of the journey.

Financial services providers

Throughout this book we will be referring to financial services companies, institutions and providers. These terms are used to refer to all of the individuals and businesses that operate in the financial services sector. This includes banks, building societies, insurance companies, pension companies, loan companies, credit card companies, financial advisers, investment companies and shares brokers among others.

Some larger institutions like the big banks will offer a wide range of services, while others specialize in particular areas of finance. Competition between these businesses is fierce and they want your custom. The advantage of this is that there are always deals on offer, even during difficult economic times. Therefore it pays to shop around.

Financial services companies often change their tactics when it comes to marketing and attracting new customers. During the early 1990s it was all about 'customer loyalty' as the providers would offer loyal customers better deals. At the moment their focus seems to be on 'new business', which means they are marketing to customers who have never used them before. This means that it pays to switch as you will get a better deal as a new customer. There is advice on shopping around and **switching** in Chapter 9.

It is also worth mentioning that alongside the well-known businesses, the financial services sector does attract its fair share of less reputable businesses. For example, there are lots of small unlicensed businesses and individuals that offer expensive loans to people who cannot get a **loan** elsewhere. These are commonly known as 'loan sharks'. Also there are scams such as 'boiler room scams' where you will be offered amazing deals on company **shares**. Therefore you have to exercise some caution. There is more information on this in Chapter 9.

> ### Insight
> The financial services sector in the UK employs an estimated 1 million people, accounts for 8% of the output of the UK as a whole and generates 8% of all tax revenues. There is an estimated £10 trillion worth of investments coming in to or going out of the UK annually. In other words, it's big business.

The financial climate

It is worth remembering that businesses in the financial services sector have to operate within the prevailing economic conditions like any other business. From 1997 to 2007 we had what some observers called a 'golden decade' with:

▶ *low unemployment: lots of people had jobs and felt confident that their jobs were safe*
▶ *low interest rates: it was cheap to borrow money*
▶ *low inflation: the price of most goods and services stayed roughly the same year after year*
▶ *house price inflation: the price of houses was going up much higher than inflation or wage increases.*

The net result of all of this was that people were borrowing lots of money to buy houses and other things. There was plenty of money in the **economy** and people were feeling confident.

In 2008, the **'credit crunch'** hit, which in turn led to a **recession**. The net result of this was that it was much harder to borrow money so people were unable to get mortgages. Therefore the housing market stalled. At the same time, consumer spending on other things like cars and holidays went down which led to job losses in those industries. This led to **unemployment** going up again and people in work becoming nervous about their job prospects, in turn meaning they spent less.

If you were a victim of this you may have lost your job or your house. However, it is important to take the longer term view here, as this is nothing new. The economy as a whole tends to follow a cycle. We have had recessions in the 1970s, 1980s and 1990s. Economists sometimes call this the 'boom–bust' cycle in that we have several years of good times followed by a year or two of bad times. The difficulty is that we don't know when the cycles will happen or how long they will last.

Having said that, once you are aware of this, you can adjust your financial habits accordingly. For example:

▶ *If you think house prices are going to fall because we are in recession, it might not be a good time to buy a house.*
▶ *If there are lots of job losses happening it is not a good time to take on more debts.*
▶ *If interest rates are low, it might be a good time to borrow money.*

Interest rates

Interest rates are important to us because they indicate how much extra we have to pay back when borrowing money. They also indicate how much we will earn on our savings. The interest rates in the UK are currently set by the Bank of England rather than the government. In very simple terms, the Bank of England controls the money supply in the UK and use interest rates as a tool to manipulate the economy:

▶ *If they think the economy is in recession they will lower the interest rates to encourage people to borrow more and therefore spend more.*

▶ *If they think there is too much activity in the economy they will increase interest rates to get us to borrow less and therefore spend less.*

The Bank of England sets the **'Base Rate'**, which is the amount they charge the banking system when they lend them money. The banks then charge us a different rate so that they can make money. The interest rates that the banks offer us when we borrow money is called the APR (Annual Percentage Rate) and when we save money is called the AER (Annual Equivalent Rate). In order for the banks to make money from us:

▶ *The APR will be higher than the Base Rate. For example, if the Base Rate is 1% we will be offered 5% so that the bank makes 4%.*
▶ *The AER will be lower than the Base Rate. For example, if the Base Rate is 1% we will be offered 0.5% so that the bank makes 0.5%.*

There is more on APR and AER in Chapters 3 and 4 respectively.

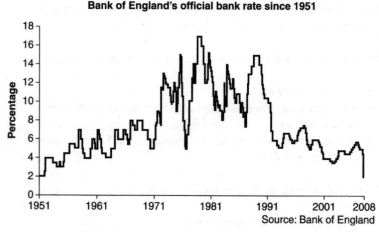

Bank of England's official bank rate since 1951

Source: Bank of England

The chart shows interest rates are changed to stimulate the economy. The dips in the 1970s, 1980s, 1990s and in 2008 are where interest rates have been lowered due to recession.

Attitudes to money

Money is a very emotive issue and our approach to it depends on our own personal beliefs and attitudes. In money terms a lot of this comes down to how much time and effort we want to put into it and our attitude to risk.

In terms of time and energy it can be difficult. Making financial decisions, shopping around, buying a financial product and then keeping up-to-date to make sure you always have the best deal can be very time-consuming. This might be time better spent enjoying life! The amount of time you spend doing this depends to an extent on the product. You might expect to spend a lot of time sorting out a **mortgage**, pension or investment, whereas buying **travel insurance** or switching credit cards might only take a few minutes.

A rule of thumb might be to look at how much time you think it will take to shop around or switch and how much money you might save. If you spend hours shopping around to save a tenner, it's probably not worth it. Another factor here is that with some financial products and services you are buying 'peace of mind'. For example, you might consider it time well spent sorting out your life insurance if you have dependant children.

In terms of risk, a high-risk approach to money might include:

- *not taking out insurance*
- *spending everything you earn and not worrying about the future just yet*
- *investing in shares in unknown businesses where the returns could be very high.*

A low-risk attitude to money might include:

- *insuring against all possible risks*
- *forgoing things now to save for a rainy day*
- *investing in government bonds with low rates of interest.*

Our attitudes to risk may change over time and depending on our circumstances. For example, if we have children we may become more aware of the need to take fewer risks, save more money and take out life insurance. As we get older, we become more aware of the need for safer investments that will guarantee us an income in retirement.

There are no rules of thumb that can be applied here as it becomes a personal decision. For example, high risk can often lead to high returns, especially when investing in the stock market. A 'safety conscious' person may miss out on these opportunities. Another example is that all of our successful entrepreneurs have taken significant risks. Many of them have experienced bankruptcy and had to start again. But many of us would not want to risk bankruptcy!

There is more on risk in Chapter 6 and information about bankruptcy in Chapter 10.

Choices, choices

One thing you are not short of when it comes to financial services is choice. This level of competition between providers is generally a good thing for us as consumers as it means there are always deals on offer. However, it also presents us with a number of problems:

- ▶ *We don't have the time to research every deal on offer.*
- ▶ *The deals change so often that we can never be sure we are on the best deal.*
- ▶ *It is difficult to compare like with like as the providers bundle their offers together in different ways.*
- ▶ *Just because a provider has done well in the past, e.g. with investments, does not mean they will in the future.*
- ▶ *Providers keep inventing new products or variations on existing products.*
- ▶ *It can be difficult to get truly impartial advice.*

This book will help you navigate the minefield of financial products and services explaining the different types of products and whether they might be suitable for your circumstances. It does not have all the answers as many of these decisions are subjective – it's called 'personal' finance for a reason. However, it will provide you with information, advice and further references so that you can be fully informed about any financial decision you make.

1

Budgeting

In this chapter you will learn:
- *what a budget is*
- *how to create a budget plan*
- *how to use your budget plan on an ongoing basis*
- *how to stick to your budget*
- *what problems you might have when budgeting and what you can do about them*
- *what cash flow is and how you can manage it*
- *how to set up a budget plan on your computer*

What is budgeting?

Budgeting is the process of creating a **budget plan**. A budget plan is a record of all the money coming in to and out of your household. In budgeting terms, all the money coming in is referred to as **income** and all the money going out is called **expenses** or **spending**.

WHY SHOULD YOU DO A BUDGET?

▶ *In most households it is quite common for the expenses to be higher than income. This is because we tend to want to buy more things than we can afford. Creating a budget will help you to keep track of your spending to stop this happening.*
▶ *People often don't realize how much they are spending or tend to underestimate the amount that they spend. Creating a budget will help you to work out the actual amount you spend.*

- *How often have you said: 'I don't know where all my money goes'? Creating a budget plan helps you to break down all of your spending into categories so you can analyse exactly how much you are spending on different things.*
- *You might get a shock when you create your budget plan and find that you are spending too much money on some things or even paying for things you don't use.*
- *Budgeting can save you money.*

Insight

Mr and Mrs A were paying £17.99 a month for broadband services with free calls to landline phones. That sounded like a reasonable deal. When they created a budget plan they found that in addition to the fixed fee, they were paying an additional £80 on average each month on calls to mobile phones. By cutting back on these calls they were able to save £40 per month.

Creating a budget plan

Creating a budget plan is not a difficult process, but it might take you a few hours to set one up. If you can, it is recommended that you create your budget plan on a computer. This is because your plan will be changing all the time and it will be easier to update on a computer – and it will do all the adding up for you. There are more details on how to do this later in this chapter.

However, the first step is to rifle through all of your financial paperwork so that you can work out exactly how much you spend on things. A good starting point is to get your bank statements from the last few months. In most households, all of the expenses will be recorded in these statements as they record all of your direct debits, standing orders, payments by cheque and cards, direct payments, cash withdrawals and repayments of credit cards and loans.

If you pay for things using direct debits, budgeting is a bit easier as you will already know how much you are paying each month for most of your bills. If you pay your bills in full when they arrive then it would be handy to have the last few bills in front of you too.

When setting up a budget you have to do it using a fixed unit of time. For example, if you are paid weekly, it makes sense to create a weekly budget plan. If you are paid monthly, then you should create a monthly budget plan.

Before you start a full budget plan, take a look at the stripped down version of a monthly plan below:

Income		
Wages	£	1,550
Family Tax Credit	£	40
Family Allowance	£	90
Total Income	£	1,680

Here you put the total amount of money coming in to the house every month from all sources. Make sure that you use the **net** figure from your salary after tax has been paid. There is more information on this in Chapter 8.

Add it all up to find your Total Income.

Expenses		
Rent/Mortgage	£	500
Council Tax	£	70
Gas	£	40
Electricity	£	40
Water Rates	£	30
Telephone/Broadband	£	40
Etc. etc.	£	
Total Expenses	£	1,600
Amount Left	£	80

In this section you have to list everything that you spend your money on. Some of these are fixed expenses like your mortgage and council tax. Other expenses will vary from month to month. Sadly, this will be a much longer list than shown in this example!

Add them all up to find your Total Expenses.

This is:
Total Income – Total Expenses

In this case:
Total Income £1,680 – Total Expenses £1,600 = £80

This means that this family has £80 left over each month. If the 'Amount Left' is a minus number it means that you are overspending. More on this later.

So you can see that the process is quite simple. The difficult bit is having the right figures available to you. In most cases you can get this information from your bank statements. For example, this family have set up direct debits or standing orders for their mortgage, council tax and utility bills so they know exactly how much they have each month.

Where you don't have a set monthly payment like a direct debit or standing order you need to work out the average amount that it costs each month. For example, if you don't pay your gas bill by direct debit you need to know (from your current gas bills) how much it costs you each year. You can then divide this by 12 and use this in your budget plan. For example, if your gas bill for the year is £600, then £600/12 means that on average you will be paying £50 a month on gas.

Paying bills in this way can cause you to have cash flow problems. There is more on this later in the chapter.

Finally, before you do your own budget plan, you need to be very honest about where the money is going. So far we have just looked at the fixed expenses, but what about those expenses that vary every month. For example, your petrol and food bills may vary a bit from month to month. The amount you spend on clothes, eating out, going to the pub etc. might vary quite a lot. Don't fool yourself! Work out exactly how much you think you spend on absolutely everything. If you are not sure, you should put in your best guess and then you might consider keeping a spending diary for a few weeks to get a more accurate figure.

Insight

Mr and Mrs B budgeted £100 a week for food, as this was the typical amount that they spent in the supermarket when they did their main shopping trip. When they looked more closely they found that in addition to the main weekly shop, they were popping in to the supermarket on at least two more occasions every week to do a bit of 'top-up shopping'. Once they had added this in they found the true cost of their food was nearer to £150 a week.

Your budget plan

It's time for you to create a budget plan. Use the table below to work out all of your expenses. We have listed all the main family expenses but you may have other things that you need to add to the list. With big items, like saving for a holiday, you need to work out what the cost is each month and include it on the plan. Notice that we have left a few blank lines under 'Income' and 'Expenses' for you to list any items not on our list.

YOUR MONTHLY BUDGET PLAN

Income	Monthly (£)
Your wages	
Your partner's wages	
Benefits	
Income from investment	
Total income	

Expenses	Monthly (£)
Mortgage/rent	
Council tax	
Gas	
Electricity	
Water rates	
Phone/broadband	
TV licence	

(Contd)

Expenses	Monthly (£)
Food	
Petrol/travel	
Car insurance	
Car tax	
Car repairs and servicing	
House insurance	
Life insurance	
Loan repayments	
Credit/store card repayments	
Pension contributions	
Savings	
Childcare	
Hobbies/clubs	
Pocket money	
School dinners	
Entertainment (eating out, pub, cinema etc.)	
Cigarettes/alcohol	
Clothes/shoes	
Holidays	
10% Contingency (see below)	
Total expenses	

Amount left (Total Income – Total Expenses)	

Make sure you take account of everything. Do you subscribe to magazines? Do you have a gym membership? Are you saving up for a holiday or for another big event (wedding, party)? If so, add it in, even if it is only a small amount.

You should try to make your figures as accurate as possible but they don't have to be 100% correct. One thing about budgeting is that real life never quite happens as you planned. Perhaps there is a birthday that you forgot about and you find yourself with a £20 present to buy. Perhaps your car tyres need replacing this month and you have to find an unexpected £100.

To take account of this, you could add a **contingency** amount to your budget. As a rough rule of thumb you could add up all of your expenses and then add another 10% on top to take account of these unexpected expenses. For example, if your monthly expenses add up to £1,800, add another £180 on top (£1,800 × 10% = £180). That would make your total expenses £1,980. If something unexpected happens this month you should be able to cover it, if not then you will have £180 left.

Using your budget plan

Once you have finished doing the budget (and it might take a while to get all the figures together) you might find you are a bit shocked. Most people underestimate how much they spend so you won't be alone if you are surprised by how much you are spending. The next obvious question is what you are going to do about it.

You may find that you have money left over at the end of the month. If this is the case it might be a good idea to take this money out of your bank account and put it somewhere where it will earn a better rate of interest than your current account with the bank (see Chapter 4).

You may find that you break even at the end of each month. This means you are spending exactly what you earn and that the 'Amount Left' each month is zero. Realistically you would probably be within a few pounds either way. This is not a bad situation as it does mean that you are living within your means.

If you have a negative amount at the end of the month it means that you are spending more money than you are earning. This is common. You will probably be borrowing money to try to keep up with your expenses. This tends to be a negative cycle as by borrowing money you increase your monthly expenses, as you have to pay it back plus interest. However, there are some times in your life when you simply have to borrow money in order to get on. The trick is to make sure that your **debt** is manageable and that you are paying as little as possible when you borrow money. There is much more about this in the book primarily in Chapters 3, 9 and 10.

In simple terms there are only two things you can do to improve your situation – earn more or spend less.

Earning more means getting a better paid job or taking on extra work. We are not always in a position to do that, so for most people, improving their financial position means taking a look at the expenses to see where economies can be made. You may be able to make simple economies that will save you money, for example, taking one less trip to the shops each week, eating fewer take-aways, walking to the shops instead of driving. The problem with this approach is that it is often hard to see how making a few small economies will really impact on your finances. The beauty of budgeting is that you will be able to see how these small economies add up to larger amounts each month.

If you want to make larger economies it is worth spending much more time shopping around. Many people will shop around when buying a large item such as a new TV, but fewer of us shop around when it comes to financial services. The reason for this is that we probably find it a bit dull. However, with the advent of the Internet and with so many businesses involved in financial services, it pays to shop around and to switch between businesses when they offer better deals. There is more information on this in Chapter 9.

Insight

Mr and Mrs C always bought their house and contents insurance with the same bank that provided them with their mortgage. For years they simply renewed the policy and had never thought to shop around. This year they used a comparison website and found that they could reduce their premium by 50% for exactly the same cover.

Cash flow

One of the problems with the budgeting plan is that there are months where it all seems to be going out and other months when you don't get any bills. For example, if you pay your bills when they arrive you could get hit for the gas, electricity, water and council tax all in the same month – and then your car breaks down just to top things off. This can give you a problem with cash flow.

Cash flow refers to the amount of money you have available to you at any one time. With the previous example, all of these bills are arriving in the same month and let's imagine you have to pay £1,000 all in one go. Although you can afford it in principle, you simply don't have the £1,000 this month. In fact it might take you two or three months to be able to get £1,000 together.

This is where budgeting can help you but you do need to plan ahead. Let's take a gas bill as an example. If your typical gas bill is £300 per quarter then you need to budget £100 each month *in advance* so that when the bill arrives you have got enough money in your bank account to pay for it. You need to do this with all of your expenses.

If you can't afford to do this you need to look at other ways of paying your bills. There are some disadvantages to direct debits and standing orders (see Chapter 7) but in the main they are a good way of budgeting as everything gets broken down into monthly repayment amounts.

Find out whether it is possible to pay in monthly **instalments** for other expenses. For example, with car insurance, many companies will offer you a monthly payment scheme. These can help you with your budgeting, but they will probably charge you extra for the service. As with other financial services it is worth shopping around for the best deal.

Another option is to use a bank **overdraft** (Chapter 3) to take care of any shortfalls. Many banks offer interest-free overdrafts allowing you to spend more than you have in your bank account each month. This free facility is typically only for a few hundred pounds. You would expect to pay a fee for overdrafts of larger amounts. You do have to be careful here. If you do not arrange the overdraft you could get hit with fees amounting to several pounds every day you are **overdrawn**. You also have to keep an eye on your **bank balance** as if you go over the **overdraft limit** you would also get hit with these fees.

Although old-fashioned, one very effective way to ensure you have enough cash flow is to use the 'jar' method, sometimes called the 'envelope' method. The idea of this is that you have separate jars or envelopes into which you put cash for each expense. So you would put £100 each month in the 'gas jar/envelope' and £40 in the 'electricity jar/envelope' and so on. This way when the bill arrives you go into the appropriate jar or envelope and the money is there. You can use the principle of this method by having money in your bank account even if you don't want to physically use a jar or envelope.

Sticking to the budget

You've now completed your budget plan and perhaps come to terms with some areas of overspending! It is important to realize that this is not a one-off exercise and that you need to monitor your spending and keep your budget plan up-to-date.

You can update your budget plan as often as you like and this will depend to some extent on your personal circumstances. If your finances are very tight you may want to keep a daily track of expenditure, perhaps using the spending diary idea. Alternatively you may want to look at the plan once a week or once a month. Having taken the time and trouble to set up the budget plan in the first place, it is an easy job to keep an eye on it, especially if it is on your computer.

Once you have set up a budget you may find that you are a lot more conscious of your spending and have a heightened awareness of where your money is going. This is usually a good thing. You may find that you need to make adjustments to your plan at the end of the month, as your initial figures were not 100% accurate. Normally, budget plans get refined over the months and become more and more accurate.

However, despite our best-laid plans, life carries on happening and things change. You need to update your budget plan as these things happen and adjust your expenditure accordingly. Major life changes usually bring about major financial changes for example: leaving home; getting married; starting a family; buying a house.

If you are planning any major life events, then it makes sense to look at the impact this will have on your monthly budget plan. You can use exactly the same format, exchanging the current figures for your estimate of what you new expenses will be.

Insight

Mr and Mrs D have been married for two years. Mr D works in the IT industry and Mrs D is a teacher. They are now expecting their first child. This will mean a drop in income in the short term and possibly in the long term too. They did have repayments of £200 a month on a sports car, which has now been traded for a cheaper family car with lower repayments. The couple also plan to start an **investment trust** for their child. They do not need to move house although they will need to spend some money preparing the house for the baby. Mr D is looking for a better paid job.

Often major life events are unplanned and these can be more difficult to cope with financially. Sadly, some of these can be the most difficult times of our lives. For example, we may find ourselves unable to work through illness. We may find ourselves caring for an ill or elderly relative. We may be made redundant. It is possible to make short- and long-term plans for these eventualities and there is more on this in Chapter 7.

Setting up a budget plan on your computer

This final section will show you how you can set up a budget plan on your computer. There are some ready-made budget tools that you can use and these are available on the Internet. You may like to try these:

- http://www.moneymadeclear.fsa.gov.uk/tools.aspx? Tool=budget_calculator
- http://www.moneysavingexpert.com/banking/ Budget-planning#bplanner
- http://www.thisismoney.co.uk/household-budget-calculator

If you have reasonable computer skills, it is worth setting up your own **spreadsheet**. The advantage of setting up your own is that you can have it exactly how you want it. It's a good idea to keep your budget plans as simple as possible. If they are simple to use you are more likely to keep them up-to-date.

You can set up a very simple but effective budget plan using Microsoft **Excel**. It may take a little while to set up, but once you have done it you can update it every month with minimal effort. You will need to set up a couple of calculations (formula) but you only have to do these once and then all the maths will be done automatically.

In the following example you can see that column A has been used to list all of the Income and Expenses and column B has been used to put in all of the amounts.

There are three formulae used:

The first is in cell B5 and adds up the Total Income:
Type this in as =(B2:B3)

The second is in cell B27 and adds up the Total Expenses:
Type this in as =SUM(B8:B25)

If you want to add a 10% contingency to the total in cell B27:
Type this in as
=SUM(B8:B25)*1.1

The third is in cell B29 and works out how much money is left:
Type this in as =B5–B27

Depending on your Excel skills you might want to tidy up the layout and format.

Once this is set up all you need to do each month is add, remove or change the figures as appropriate.

	A	B	C
1	**Income**		
2	Wages	£1,995.00	
3	Family Allowance	£ 120.00	
4			
5	Total Income	£2,115.00	
6			
7	**Expenses**		
8	Rent	£ 550.00	
9	Council Tax	£ 160.00	
10	Water	£ 30.00	
11	Gas	£ 60.00	
12	Electricity	£ 63.00	
13	Telephone	£ 55.00	
14	Pocket money	£ 40.00	
15	Music lessons	£ 80.00	
16	Savings	£ 50.00	
17	Life Insurance	£ 40.00	
18	TV Licence	£ 12.00	
19	Petrol	£ 160.00	
20	Food	£ 400.00	
21	Loan	£ 165.00	
22	Charity	£ 50.00	
23	DVD Rental	£ 13.00	
24	Entertainment	£ 150.00	
25	Bank Account Charges	£ 12.00	
26			
27	Total Expenses	£2,090.00	
28			
29	**Amount left**	£ 25.00	
30			
31			

Microsoft Excel - Budget Plan.XLS

File Edit View Insert Format Tools Data Window Help

B5 =SUM(B2:B3)

TEN IMPORTANT THINGS TO REMEMBER

1 *It is vital to complete a budget plan, which is a record of all the money coming in and going out of the household.*

2 *Budgeting can save you money by highlighting areas where you are over-spending.*

3 *Most households underestimate the amount of money that they spend.*

4 *You will need recent bank statements to be able to complete your budget.*

5 *You need to watch your cash flow over the month, which means having the money available when you need it.*

6 *Paying bills monthly by direct debit or standing order makes it easier to budget and manage cash flow.*

7 *You need to be very honest when completing your budget plan and take account of everything that you spend.*

8 *If you end up with a negative amount on your budget plan you either need to earn more or spend less!*

9 *You have to revise your budget on a regular basis as things change.*

10 *It can be helpful to use a computer spreadsheet to do your budgets.*

2

Children and students

In this chapter you will learn:

- *how much it costs to bring up children*
- *what a Child Trust Fund (CFT) is and the different types on offer*
- *how to set up investments for your children*
- *ways of paying for childcare and school fees*
- *what Educational Maintenance Allowance (EMA) is and how to claim it*
- *how to arrange a gap year*
- *what student finance is available in terms of loans, grants and bank accounts*

Introduction

Let's start with some scary statistics. A recent survey by financial services provider Liverpool and Victoria (now called LV) estimated that the average cost of bringing up a child from birth to age 21 is around £180,000. Their research also found that around £50,000 of this is on childcare and education, based on using the state education system. This total goes up significantly to around £250,000 if you send your offspring to private school. To put that into some kind of perspective, you will be spending around £8,500 per year on each of your children. That's around £23.50 a day so only the price of a reasonably priced pub meal for two!

In this chapter we will be looking at each of the key stages in children's lives from birth through to university.

Child Trust Funds (CTFs) and investments

The **Child Trust Fund (CTF)** is a government-backed savings scheme designed to give every child a small **lump sum** to start off a savings account. The hope is that it will encourage parents to set up savings accounts for their children, which will then get topped up regularly. It is also hoped that as the child gets older they will start to take an interest in their own savings.

Every child born after 1 September 2002 receives a voucher worth £250, or £500 for low income families. Parents need to open a CTF account to pay the money in and can then top up the account either on a regular basis or on occasions when their child receives other money, for example birthday money. On the child's seventh birthday they receive an additional £250, or again £500 for low income families, to put into the account. The money can be taken out by the child on reaching their 18th birthday.

The current tax rules are that you can pay in up to £1,200 a year tax free. This means that there will be no tax to pay on the interest received from the account.

Insight

Mr and Mrs A opened a CTF account for their five-year-old son when he was born. The account has been paying around 3% AER and they have paid in the maximum tax free amount each year. Over a period of five years they have generated savings of over £6,000 and have saved over £50 in tax. The tax saving might not sound like a lot, but it is £50 that goes to their son rather than the tax office.

The numbers soon add up if you are able to pay in the tax-free amount. £1,200 is £100 a month so you need to think about how affordable this might be based on your budget. However, by doing this you would be looking at generating a nest-egg of over £25,000 for your child on their 18th birthday (assuming an AER of 3%). Obviously this will vary depending on which account you choose and what happens to interest rates over time.

The average amount that a parent pays in to a child savings account is estimated at £30 a month. Added to the £500 government money, if you did this you could be looking at a total of around £10,000 for their 18th birthday.

If you want to know more details about the Child Trust Fund go to the government website: http://www.childtrustfund.gov.uk/

In common with many financial services you will be able to choose from a wide range of banks and other institutions that offer CTF accounts. You will need to shop around for the best deal at the time, particularly in terms of interest rates, which are constantly changing. You also need to make a choice based on your attitude to risk. A quick Internet search for 'CTF accounts' will give you at least 50 to choose from. The website above also gives a list of providers. There are three main types of account:

Savings account: this is a standard accounts where you pay in your money and you will receive interest. The amount of interest is shown as the AER (Average Equivalent Rate). In simple terms the higher the AER the more interest you will receive on your savings. You may find that the AER is lower on these types of accounts but it is guaranteed and therefore these are low-risk investments.

Accounts that invest in shares: these are accounts where the savings are invested in the stock market. The performance of these accounts vary and will depend on how well the stock market is doing. You will also have to pay a charge to the provider for the running of the account. On the plus side, the amount your savings earn can be much higher than a standard savings account. On the down side, you could end up with less than you paid in. Whether you choose one of these depends on your attitude to risk. You also need to think about your investment over the long term (see the next Insight box).

Stakeholder account: these are accounts where the savings get invested in the stock market, but the investments are spread across several companies to spread the risk. The government has set strict rules as to how the money can be invested to minimize the risk of loss. As the child gets older, the savings are moved into less risky investments. There is also a charge payable for running this account but it is a regulated amount.

Insight

Mr and Mrs D set up a CTF account that invested in shares. They are taking the long view in that they know that the money cannot be taken out of the account until their child reaches 18. At the time they knew that the stock market was not performing well but took the view that over a period of years the fluctuations should even out. Therefore, in the early stages they are investing in shares that carry a higher risk. When their child reaches 10 they are planning to move towards safer share choices.

Childcare

This has become a thorny issue for many people over recent years. The majority of families in this country now have both parents going out to work either full or part-time. Parents obviously still provide a large part of the childcare and other family members are increasingly becoming unpaid carers.

In other circumstances, however, families are paying for professional childcare and there are a number of options here. The costs can vary enormously depending on what form of childcare you choose and even where you live. Whichever way you look at it, it becomes a juggling act and almost a 'catch-22': the more you work the more you earn but the more childcare you need; the less you work, the less you earn but the less childcare you will need. Your final decision may not of course be a financial one and this chapter makes no attempt to cover the non-financial aspects of choosing the best childcare for your circumstances. That would need a book all of its own!

It may be helpful to work out the annual costs of the different forms of childcare as this then gives you an easy comparison against your annual salary in terms of affordability, or indeed, how much you need or want to work.

According to the Daycare Trust charity (www.daycaretrust.org.uk):

▶ *The typical cost of a full-time nursery place for a child under two is £167 a week in England. This is significantly higher in London and the south-east, where it could rise to over £220 per week. That's between £8,684 and £11,440 a year.*
▶ *The typical weekly cost of a full-time place with a childminder for a child under two in England is £156. That's over £8,000 a year.*
▶ *The typical cost for an after school club is around £40 for 15 hours. That's just over £2,000 a year.*
▶ *The typical cost of a place for a child in a summer play scheme is around £90 a week. That's £540 assuming a 6-week school holiday.*

Another option is the live-in nanny, which can cost between £150 and £400 a week depending on where you live and how much you expect them to do. Annually that comes to between £7,800 and £20,800.

Some help is available from the government in terms of free nursery places and there is some financial help through the tax system. Three- and four-year-olds are entitled to a part-time place in a nursery or other establishment. Many schools have early education systems usually starting from the age of four.

You may be eligible for the childcare element of the Working Tax Credit. The average amount is £65 a week.

The tax rules change every year so it is always worth checking the appropriate websites. The Daycare Trust have a website dedicated to financial help available for parents (www.payingforchildcare.org.uk) or you can get the latest information from the government website (www.direct.gov.uk/en/Parents/Childcare).

School fees

The choice of school for your child is one of the biggest decisions you make in your life, so no pressure! This section will focus on the financial aspects of this only. Before you start to look at the cost of financing private education, it is worth considering how good your local state schools are and whether your child can get into them. You might consider that moving into the catchment area of a good state school is more cost effective than going private. The Ofsted website (www.ofsted.gov) contains inspection reports for every state school and nursery in the country. This details their academic achievement and how they deal with the personal and social development of your child.

In terms of private education, according to the Independent School Council (www.isc.co.uk), typical costs are just over £3,000 a term for a day student and just over £7,000 for a boarder. This will vary enormously depending on the type and status of the school. Preparatory schools are usually less expensive starting at £2,000 a term.

Fees are normally payable a term in advance. You need to plan for this both in terms of having the available funds but also in terms of allowing for a term's notice if you were to move your child. Looking longer term you need to budget for school fees so that you cover the whole of your child's education. You also need to factor in other additional costs such as uniforms, sports gear, extra-curricular activities (e.g. music lessons) and trips.

Bursaries, scholarships and **grants** may be available depending on your personal circumstances. Bursaries and scholarships are usually offered by the schools themselves and are used to attract students who show particular potential or have specific financial difficulties. Some of these awards will be means-tested. Grants are usually from organizations such as charities with a specific agenda. More information about grants is available from www.cafonline.org/. Bursaries, scholarships and grants are sometimes available to cover the entire cost of a child's education but more commonly they will provide part of the cost and there are often conditions attached.

In a competitive market you may find that school fees are negotiable, particularly if you have more than one child at the same school. Some schools will offer further discounts for paying well in advance, e.g. more than a term ahead. Typically, if you educate you child privately from nursery onwards you can expect to spend somewhere between £90,000 and £120,000 over their time at school. The figure is higher if they board and if they stay on in the sixth form. It's perhaps worth remembering that they could spend up to 15 years in school.

How you fund this depends on how well you have planned for it. If you have planned from your child's birth you may have the luxury of using savings. Many parents release **equity** from their house by extending their mortgage. If you are over 50 you may be able to draw on your pension and continue to work. In most cases, private education is largely funded through your earnings, or a combination of all of the above.

Insight

Mr and Mrs W sent their children to school in South Africa. They considered that the standard of education was comparable with UK schools and were impressed with the school's emphasis on school spirit and manners. The fees were significantly lower than UK schools although the cost of flying out to see their children four times a year did have to be factored in.

Educational Maintenance Allowance (EMA)

EMA is an allowance specifically designed to encourage students to stay on for extra full-time study when they are aged 16 to 19. The student can claim between £10 and £30 a week during term-time. The actual amount you get is based on the household income. The figures for courses starting in September 2009 are shown below. You can check the latest figures at http://ema.direct.gov.uk/ where you can also find more detailed information and apply.

Household income	EMA payment
Up to £20,817 per year	£30 per week
£20,818–£25,521 per year	£20 per week
£25,522–£30,810 per year	£10 per week
More than £30,810	No entitlement to EMA

You have to have the money paid direct into a bank account set up for the student and regular attendance and satisfactory progress need to be made. EMA does not affect any benefits that you may be claiming as parents and you child is allowed to earn money part-time in addition to the EMA.

Gap years

Figures published recently by *The Times* newspaper estimate that around 240,000 people aged between 18 and 24 take a gap year, spending between £3,000 and £4,000. Gap years can be of significant advantage to a young person's job and career prospects so this money may be well-spent. At the time of writing, the Department for International Development was funding gap years for students from less well-off backgrounds through http://myplatform2.com.

Many students do not take a full year but will work for several months to put the money together and then have several months travelling.

Alternatively, young people can obtain visas to work (if necessary) as they travel taking on anything from bar work to fruit picking.

Charity gap years are increasingly popular where students do not expect to get paid for the work they do. There is often a commitment to raise a certain amount of money before the student can travel.

You do need to be a bit careful these days in that there are now so many young people taking gap years that many businesses have seen a marketing opportunity offering gap year experiences for young people, which are nothing more than expensive holidays. Travelling independently or for charity is usually much cheaper and more rewarding.

Costs to factor in include the obvious such as travel, accommodation and food, and perhaps the less obvious including insurance and impact of exchange rates. Round-the-world flights are available which work out much cheaper than individual flights. These are normally based on the number of stops and start from around £600 for five stops. You have to factor in taxes, which will probably double this amount. The good old-fashioned Europe inter-rail experience is still as popular as ever with train travel available around most countries in Europe from £150.

Accommodation can vary from a tent to a friend's or relative's sofa to hostels specifically designed for young travellers. Facilities are usually very good in the latter with the downside being that you are often sharing a room. Prices in Europe can be as low as 10 euros a night but this will vary as with any other form of holiday accommodation. Most hostels can be viewed and booked over the Internet prior to travel.

Student loans

The student loan system has been under constant review over recent years mainly due to the fact that over 40% of young people now choose to stay on to do further study after the age of 18. This is a massive expense for the nation as a whole and increasingly the cost of being a student is being passed to the students themselves, or more likely, the parents. The typical cost of being a student is somewhere around £10,000 a year. This breaks down roughly evenly between tuition fees paid to the university, accommodation and living expenses. Most courses last three years so you are looking at a total bill of £30,000 per child.

Student fees have been increasing over recent years. The figure for students starting in 2009/10 was £3,225 a year. The government sets this amount each year although the universities often push to have these increased. At the time of writing some universities were pushing to set the amount at between £5,000 and £7,000 a year.

Accommodation is usually provided by the university in the first year and then students have to make their own arrangements with private landlords. The amount will vary depending on which part of the country the university is in. One advantage of using the university accommodation is that it is an all-in price for the accommodation and the **utilities** (students are currently not required to pay council tax). Typical prices in Leeds might be around £75 a week whereas in London you might expect to pay £120 a week. You are usually required to pay this every week apart from the summer holidays so you can budget to be paying this for 40–42 weeks of the year.

Living expenses again will vary depending on how expensive your offspring's tastes are! You need to think about travel, food, books, insurance and of course beer or other forms of entertainment.

There is some help available for funding and it is possible to get grants that do not have to be paid back. The rest is done through the student loan system or has to be paid for by parents. The rules and amounts vary from year to year so you need to check the latest information at: http://www.direct.gov.uk/en/EducationAndLearning/UniversityAndHigherEducation/StudentFinance/index.htm

As a quick summary:

Maintenance (or special support) **grant:** These can be worth up to £3,000 a year and may be available depending on your circumstances. Additional help may be available for older students with dependants, or disabled students. **Student grants** do not have to be paid back but are means tested. For the academic year 2009/10 the figures were:

Household income	Amount of grant
Up to £25,000	Full grant: £2,906
£30,000	£1,906
£34,000	£1,106
£40,000	£711
£45,000	£384
£50,020	£50
More than £50,020	No grant

Student loans: You can get one loan to cover the tuition fees and another for maintenance (living expenses). The amount you can borrow depends to some extent on income. The tuition fees loan will cover the full amount (around £3,200) and you can get a **maintenance loan** for around £5,000. You get slightly more or less than this depending on whether the student lives away from the family home and whether they live in London. These have lower interest rates than commercial loans (typically around 1.5%) and must be paid back at 9% of everything the student subsequently earns over £15,000 a year. After 25 years any remaining amount gets written off.

For the academic year 2009/10, the figures were as follows:

	Living at home	Living away from home outside London	Living away from home in London
Maximum student loan for maintenance	£3,838	£4,950	£6,928
72% not income assessed (to the nearest £5)	£2,763	£3,564	£4,988
Remainder (around 28%) income assessed	£1,975	£1,386	£1,940

Bursaries: These are made available by specific universities to encourage students onto particular courses. These are usually paid to students on lower incomes or other students who would otherwise not get the chance to study. Information on grants is available on the websites of each university.

As you might expect the rules all get quite complicated very quickly and there is a lot of form-filling to be done for the application process. This can be done online at the government website given above.

There is much speculation about the typical size of the student debt and if you bear in mind that they will get around £8,000 a year for fees and maintenance, plus whatever they might borrow from their bank, you can see how after three years your son/daughter could come out with more than £25,000 of debt.

In view of this many students now expect to work during term-time and holidays to partly support themselves. **Minimum wage** jobs pay just around £5 an hour for university age students. If they can average 12 hours a week during term-time they can expect to earn around £3,000, which is about a third of what they need each year. Many students concentrate on their studies during term-time and work full-time for the 12–15 weeks that they have on holidays. Many students do a bit of both, mindful of the fact that they do not want their jobs to interfere with their university work.

Student bank accounts

Banks and other financial services institutions are very sophisticated when it comes to marketing and encouraging young people to open accounts with them. They know that many young people will stick with the same bank for years and years and this is why they are keen to catch them young. One of the enticements for students is that they can be offered credit facilities from their eighteenth birthday and most banks will offer interest-free overdrafts. This means they can borrow more money than they have in the bank. Some of these offers will only last a certain amount of time and there will be strict limits. If they go over the overdraft limit they will be hit with **overdraft charges**, which may be added for every day that they are overdrawn.

It is important for your 18-year-old to realize that they are being marketed at and that banking it is a competitive market. Consequently they need to shop around for the best student bank account. The deals change all the time and are often packaged differently to make it difficult to compare one against the other.

For example, some banks offer cash incentives or other freebies such as rail cards. These may be a good idea if the offer is something that is of genuine value i.e. your son/daughter is planning to use the trains a lot. Otherwise, you are probably best looking at which account offers an interest-free overdraft for the longest period. Remember that the interest-free deal will end the day that they stop being a student and all that borrowing will then go onto a standard APR.

They should also not lose sight of the fact that they are already borrowing money on a student loan to cover their everyday expenses so the first question should be whether they really need to take on further borrowing even if it is interest free. One possible option is to take the interest-free money from the overdraft and put it into a high interest savings account. When the interest-free period ends they can pay off the overdraft and keep the money made on the interest from the savings account.

TEN IMPORTANT THINGS TO REMEMBER

1 *Each child is going to cost about £180,000 from birth to age 21.*

2 *Private education could easily push this up to £250,000.*

3 *You are entitled to £250 to set up a Child Trust Fund and can invest up to £1,200 a year tax free.*

4 *There is a range of options when it comes to childcare that could cost you nothing or up to £20,000 a year.*

5 *You may be entitled to state help with the provision and cost of childcare.*

6 *Private education costs between £2,000 and £8,000 a term. You need to plan for the whole of your child's education to avoid disruption.*

7 *Educational Maintenance Allowance (EMA) of up to £30 per week is available to many 16–19-year-olds who stay on in education.*

8 *Gap years can be a valuable experience and typically cost £3,000 to £4,000.*

9 *The typical cost of being a student is £10,000 a year for three years.*

10 *Students needs to shop around to get the best deal on their bank account.*

3

....

Borrowing money

In this chapter you will learn:
- *the principles of borrowing money including APR*
- *how to select the most appropriate type of borrowing for your situation*
- *what different types of loan are available*
- *what an overdraft is*
- *what credit, debit and ATM cards are*
- *what other types of card are available including store and loyalty cards*
- *what charges apply to borrowing money*
- *whether it is worth protecting yourself against not being able to pay off money owed using Payment Protection Insurance (PPI)*

Introduction

On the surface, borrowing money seems to be a fairly simple **transaction**. You borrow the money from an organization, usually a bank or loan company, and then you pay them back, plus interest. The repayments are usually paid monthly and are calculated so that after a certain number of months, the debt is cleared.

The amount you pay back is calculated as an **Annual Percentage Rate (APR)** and any company that lends money must by law publicize their APR prominently in their advertising and literature. In simple terms, if you borrow £1,000 for one year with an APR of 10% you will pay back £1,100, therefore paying £100 for the credit facility. Most loans last for more than one year and the APR does reflect the total amount you will pay back over the loan period.

The image below shows an extract from one of the comparison sites (www.comparethemarket.com) with the **typical APR** being prominently advertised for each provider.

Provider & product	Typical APR	Amount & term	Monthly repayment / Total amount repayable	Other Charges	More About This Loan
	?	?	?	?	
Sainsbury's Finance **Sainsbury's Finance** Personal Loan	Typical **7.9% APR**	£10,000 60 months	£200.99 / £12,059.40	No charges that we know of	DETAILS & APPLY ⟶
Alliance & Leicester A&L Exclusive Personal Loan	Typical **7.9% APR**	£10,000 60 months	£200.99 / £12,059.40	No charges that we know of	DETAILS & APPLY ⟶
HALIFAX **Halifax** Existing Customer Personal Loan	Typical **8.1% APR**	£10,000 60 months	£201.87 / £12,112.20	No charges that we know of	DETAILS & APPLY ⟶
BANK OF SCOTLAND **Bank of Scotland** Existing Customer Personal Loan	Typical **8.1% APR**	£10,000 60 months	£201.87 / £12,112.20	No charges that we know of	DETAILS & APPLY ⟶
BARCLAYS **Barclays Bank** Existing Customer Barclayloan Plus	Typical **9.9% APR**	£10,000 60 months	£209.91 / £12,594.60	No charges that we know of	DETAILS & APPLY ⟶

Best buy personal loans from lovemoney.com partners

* Example repayments based on a loan of £10,000 paid over 60 months without PPI
† The rate displayed is a lovemoney.com rate.

The APR is a very useful measure as it enables you to compare one deal against another. It also helps you to decide whether you think it is worth taking out the loan in the first place, in that you can identify how much it is costing you to get the money now, compared to waiting and saving up. You will see a 'typical APR' quoted, which is the average rate that most customers get. You may however, be charged more than this.

In common with most aspects of financial services, it is never quite that simple as the loans companies and banks have clever marketing to make it more difficult to compare like with like. Many have additional charges on top of the APR figure quoted and there are usually penalty charges if you do not stick to the terms of the agreement. Some make an additional charge if you pay off the loan early. The old adage of reading the small print could not be more accurate when it comes to borrowing money.

One thing to be aware of here is that it is far too easy to have several different lines of credit. For example, you may take out a loan for a car and a holiday, have two different credit cards, a couple of store cards and an overdraft. Any one of these debts might be quite manageable but added all together you may find that you are paying a lot for these credit facilities, whereas you might not really need them all.

Loans: secured, unsecured and consolidation

A loan is money borrowed which will be repaid for a set period at a stated APR. It sounds simple but there are lots of considerations including:

- *the amount of the loan*
- *whether secured or unsecured*
- *the period of the loan (usually measured in months)*
- *which financial services company to get it from*
- *the APR and other charges.*

Most people take out loans to pay for something in particular, for example a car, holiday or wedding. The loan can typically be repaid in anything between six months and 25 years although it is most common for loans to last between two to five years. If you need ongoing credit for everyday expenses or if you want to borrow the money for less than six months you may be better off using an overdraft facility instead.

You and the company you are borrowing from should both be satisfied that you can make the repayments. This is where your budget comes in handy as the repayments including the interest are calculated on a monthly basis. It is worth mentioning that although most loans are personal loans and based on the income of one person, it is possible to obtain joint loans, for example for couples and married people. In these cases both incomes are taken into account and both parties are responsible for repayment.

Insight

Ms S was considering taking out a loan for £10,000 to buy a new car. She wanted the loan over five years (60 months) and she was offered an APR of 10%. Using a web-based loan calculator she worked out that the monthly repayment would be £210.36. The total she would repay would be £12,621, which means she will pay £2,621 for the loan.

You can get an idea of how much loans will cost by using various independent online loan calculators. These do not give 100% accurate figures but it means you can get a rough idea without having to type all your personal details into the banking websites. The following is one website you could try:

www.moneymadeclear.fsa.gov.uk/tools/loan_calculator.html
http://www.fool.co.uk/loans/loan-calculator.aspx

A **secured loan** is one that is guaranteed against your house. The advantage of this is that the APR will be less than an unsecured loan, but it does mean that if you fail to pay the money back, the loan company can legally repossess your house in order to get the money owed. Obviously there is an element of risk in taking the secured loan. You may also find that there are restrictions on what you can use the money for. Secured loans are often used to make improvements to property in which case it makes more sense to have the loan secured against that property.

The more common type is the **unsecured personal loan** where the lending company will lend you money based on your ability to repay. In order to get the loan the bank will ask for income information from you and possibly from your partner if applicable. Some will require proof of income and will run a credit check on you where they will verify your credit history. If you have failed to make payments on loans or other credit deals in the past, you may be refused the loan, or you may be offered a lower amount, or be asked to pay a higher APR.

Once you have decided that you do want the loan and that you can afford it, you need to shop around for the best deal. There are hundreds of different organizations that will lend you money including banks and loan companies. Banks usually insist that you have a current account with them and often use cheap loans as a way of attracting customers. Once you are a customer they then have the opportunity to sell you other financial products. You may also choose a specialist loan company, most of which are reputable. You should avoid the 'loan shark' end of the market which is characterized by small businesses that lend with very high APRs.

The problem is that the banks only tend to lend to people with good credit histories. This means people who have borrowed money before and paid it back. Basically, the worse your **credit history** is the harder you will find it to borrow money and the higher your APR will be. This is because all lending decisions are based on the credit history of the borrower. There is more on this in Chapter 9.

You can use price comparison websites to find the cheapest loan or it may simply be a case of approaching your own bank. You can apply online, by phone or in a branch and decisions are usually made within a few minutes. If approved the funds will be transferred into your current account within a couple of days and you will be asked to set up a direct debit, which they will start to take out almost immediately. You may find it useful to ask for the direct debit date to be the same as other payments so that you have all of your main expenses leaving the account at the same time (ideally a couple of days after you get paid).

Consolidation loans are loans that you take out in order to pay off existing loans. There are circumstances where such a loan might be beneficial, but you have to proceed with caution on these. Daytime TV is full of adverts for loan companies that offer this facility and your bank may also be happy to offer it too. The idea is if you have several loans or other forms of credit agreement, these companies will pay them all off by giving you one big loan that covers the lot. They will arrange to pay off the other companies and you simply pay a monthly amount for the new consolidation loan.

Two good reasons to take one of these loans are:

▶ *You feel your borrowing is in a mess and you want to put it all into one monthly payment.*
▶ *You are offered a lower APR on the consolidation loan than you are paying on your other borrowing.*

However, you need to be careful as these loans can appear cheap because the companies will reduce your total monthly payments. They are only usually able to do this by spreading the loan over a longer period, so in the long run you will pay more. They will also charge an **arrangement fee**, and this may not be reflected in the APR quoted.

Overdrafts

An overdraft is a short-term lending facility provided by your bank on your current account. It means that you can spend more money than you have got. For example, the bank may provide an overdraft facility of £1,000 so the balance of your account can get to –£1,000 before you have to stop spending. Many banks will offer an interest-free overdraft up to a certain amount. After that the bank will charge interest on the overdraft and this amount is usually quoted as a monthly APR. If you multiply this by 12 you will get an idea of how much it is costing compared to other forms of finance.

There is a distinction to make here between a **planned overdraft**, where you organize it with the bank in advance, and an **unplanned overdraft** where you simply over-spend during the month.

If you do go overdrawn and do not make arrangements with the bank there are likely to be charges, which can be very high and may be added for every day you are overdrawn. The advice therefore if you are going to have an overdraft is to plan for it and arrange it with the bank. If you accidently go overdrawn, contact your bank immediately to sort it out.

Many people use planned overdrafts to cover shortfalls in cash flow. For example, you may have a bad month where all the bills arrive and your car breaks down. You plan to be straight again by the time you get paid again, so you just use the overdraft for the month. This is a sensible and cost-effective way around the problem.

Other people are always running on their overdraft and this is less sensible as you are paying every month for this facility just so that you can meet all your living expenses. If this is the case, you need to look carefully at your budget to see if you are simply living beyond your means. It may be more sensible to get a small loan to get you back in credit and then get rid of the overdraft altogether. You do however have to be careful not to get into a cycle of loans and overdrafts as in the case study below.

Insight

Mr and Mrs R have three small children. Mr R works full-time and Mrs R part-time. Although both are in safe jobs, it is a constant struggle to make ends meet and there are often unexpected expenses associated with having children. The family has been running on an overdraft of just under £2,000 a month. This means that every time they get paid, the balance only just goes above zero. To get back into credit the family has taken a **personal loan** for £2,000. This has increased their monthly outgoings by £200. Within six months the family found that their overdraft was approaching £2,000 again and they were still paying off the loan.

Credit, debit and ATM cards

These days we all need big wallets and purses just to keep all our plastic in. This section aims to explain the cards that we get from the bank and the next section looks at those available in shops.

Credit cards allow you to spend money you haven't got. On application for a card you will be credit checked and if successful, given a card limit. You can then use the card as much as you like until you hit the limit. Sometimes the limit will be higher than the actual limit you want so you may be tempted to spend more than you planned on your credit card. If you go over the limit, your card will be refused when you try to use it, or some companies will allow you to go over by a small amount subject to a charge.

Credit cards charge an APR which allows you to compare one deal to another. Many will offer zero per cent interest for a few months before reverting to a variable rate. Other cards offer other incentives such as cash back. In common with other aspects of finance, this is a very competitive market and the credit card companies are always looking for ways to get you to switch and to make it difficult to compare deals! If you do switch, you need to watch out for switching fees, which are quoted as a percentage of the balance that you are transferring to the new card. As the rates are variable it means that your credit card company can put them up (or down) at any time.

Typically you have a month to pay off the outstanding amount before interest is charged. The typical APR at the time of writing is 15%, making the cost of using the card slightly higher than taking out a loan. If you are organized and pay off the amount each month then credit cards are great as they give you the convenience of not having to carry cash, and they don't cost you anything. They also have the added advantage of purchase protection insurance, which means that anything you buy with your credit card is automatically insured against accidental damage or theft.

The disadvantages come if you do not pay back the full amount each month. In this case you will be paying the interest charges and you also have to be careful of penalty charges for either going over your limit, or not paying back the minimum monthly amount. These charges are often very high.

It is also possible to withdraw cash using a credit card. This is an expensive way of borrowing as you do not get the interest-free period that you would with other credit card transactions. The interest is charged from the day that you take the money out. Some credit card companies have a higher APR for cash.

It is also possible to use a credit card cheque. You can use these like normal cheques but the credit card company charge you in the same way as if you were making a cash withdrawal using your credit card. This means that you pay interest straight away on the amount of the cheque. In addition, many companies charge a handling fee, which is typically 2.5% of the value of the cheque.

Credit card cheques are controversial because the credit card companies used to send blank cheques to customers when they hadn't asked for them. This was seen as irresponsible as it was encouraging people to spend money they did not have. The government are banning this practice although credit card cheques are still available to those who wish to use them.

Using credit card cheques or withdrawing cash on your credit card are both expensive ways of borrowing. If you find yourself doing this a lot, it may be a sign that you are not budgeting properly. If you are using these methods to borrow money over longer periods then you would be better off looking at other types of borrowing that have lower APRs.

Insight

Mr J used his credit card when he was paying for holidays or higher value items such as electrical equipment. He did this as the card gave him insurance cover on what he bought.

(Contd)

He was usually very good at paying off the full amount at the end of each month. On one occasion due to being in holiday he missed a payment. He incurred a £12 charge for the missed payment, a £12 charge for going over his limit, and was taken off his 0% deal as he had not kept to the terms of his credit agreement, therefore having to pay 15.9% on the total amount owed.

Debit cards vary from credit cards in that when you pay for something, you must have the funds in your bank, or an overdraft facility to cover the spending. If the funds are not available the card will be refused and you will be embarrassed at the checkout. Many people prefer debit cards for budgeting reasons in that you can only spend what you have got in the bank or at the most, up to your overdraft limit. However, debit cards do not have the insurance protection offered by credit cards, and they do not usually attract any other incentives or freebies.

ATM cards are those that can only be used for withdrawing cash from cash machines. Like debit cards, you have to have the funds available in your bank account. These are not as common as the credit and debit cards. Some people opt for ATM cards as a way of controlling their spending as it means that they cannot be tempted into buying something in a shop, unless they have the cash with them.

Store cards, loyalty cards and in-store finance deals

A **store card** is basically a credit card which you can use in one particular shop or chain of shops. They work in exactly the same way as a credit card in that you do not have to pay straight away, but can settle the debt either all in one go before the end of the month, or by paying a regular amount.

There is one school of thought that you should never ever have a store card or take any of the credit deals that you get offered in shops. The reason for this is that the APR on these deals is usually very high. Typical APRs at the time of writing were around 20–30% compared to a typical APR on a credit card of 15%.

The way this works is that when you buy something from a shop you will be offered a discount on your purchase if you sign up for the store card. You may also be offered other benefits for taking the card. You will be credit checked and if that comes back OK, you get your card with a credit limit on it. You can make purchases up to the value of that limit. Typically you will not be charged interest if you pay back what you owe on the card within one month. Therefore, if you are sure that you will do this, the card can be a good deal as it is not costing you anything and you got the discount on your original purchase.

However, if you do not have the funds or if you are not organized enough to remember to pay off the outstanding amount each month, you will start to be charged these high rates of interest on what you owe. If you only make the minimum payment required you will end up paying significantly more for your products than paying up front.

Loyalty cards differ slightly in that they do not initially have any credit on them until you have built it up. They are effectively rewards schemes where points are added to the card every time you buy something. These build up and allow you to get discounts from further purchases. They were invented for the benefit of the retailer as they give them a very accurate record of everything you have ever bought. This then helps them with their marketing. The advantage for us is that they do lead to discounts, particularly if you are a regular customer.

In addition to the store cards, many retailers will offer **finance deals**. In the old days we used to call these hire purchase agreements. These are usually for higher value purchases and are effectively just loans. The difference is that the loan is for the specific item being purchased. Stores are often keen to get you to buy things on credit as they make money on the finance deal as well as selling you the item.

In common with other credit arrangements they must quote the APR so that you have a clear idea of how much the credit is costing. In a competitive market, many businesses will offer 0% finance deals, which means you are paying nothing at all for the credit. You might find that products with 0% finance are more expensive as they have added the cost to the item! The best advice is to shop around and to add up the total cost of the item and the credit before you make your decision. If you can afford to buy it outright then there is not much point in paying for the credit.

Another thought is that technically, you do not own the item until the final payment is made so in theory if you do not keep up repayments the store can repossess the item.

APR and other charges

As we have seen in this chapter, the APR is the most important factor when looking at how much credit costs. However, there are often additional costs for arranging finance deals and almost always penalty charges if you fail to stick to a credit agreement. The table on pages 45–46 summarizes the typical costs for each of the types of finance deal that we have looked at.

Type of finance	Typical APR	Additional charges	Penalty charges
Loan	8–15%	Arrangement fees, particularly for consolidation or secured loans – typically 1–5% of loan value.	**Early repayment penalties** – you may have to pay a proportion of the total interest if you pay off the loan early. Recovery fees for late or non-payment. Your home is at risk if loans are secured against your property.
Overdraft	15–20%	Higher interest rates charged on unauthorized overdrafts.	Daily charges on unauthorized overdrafts – up to £40 per instance. Recovery fees for late or non-payment.
Credit card	12–20%	Commission payable on cash withdrawals from ATMs or credit card cheques – up to 3% of transaction. No interest-free period on cash withdrawals. **Transaction fees** if used abroad – up to 3% of transaction.	Late payment and overdue fees up to £12 per instance. Over-limit fees for exceeding the credit limit up to £12 per instance. *[Contd]*

Type of finance	Typical APR	Additional charges	Penalty charges
		Annual or monthly membership fees on some cards. Fee charged for transferring a balance from other credit cards – typically 3–5%.	
Store card	20–30%		Late payment and overdue fees up to £25 per instance. Over-limit fees for exceeding the credit limit up to £25 per instance.
In-store finance	0–30%	Arrangement fees only usually payable for customers with poor credit ratings.	Early repayment penalties – you may have to pay a proportion of the total interest if you pay off the loan early. Recovery fees for late or non-payment.

Payment Protection Insurance (PPI)

Whenever you are borrowing money you will probably be offered, and should consider, **Payment Protection Insurance (PPI)**. The idea of this is that if you cannot make the repayments for certain reasons, usually accident, illness or unemployment, then the insurance will cover the repayments or part of them for a set period of time. The insurance **premium** is either added to the monthly repayments or can be paid as a lump sum. If it is added to the amount you borrow, then you will pay interest on the PPI payment.

You can buy PPI from the company that you are borrowing the money from or you can shop around and buy it independently in which case you may get a better deal.

You should not feel pressurized into buying PPI and you should never be refused a loan because you do not take the cover. The main question to ask yourself is that if you were unable to earn money through no fault of your own, then would you be able to afford to keep up the payments on all of your borrowing. This means all of your debts and not just this one.

A good rule of thumb here is to look at your monthly budget and to make sure that you have enough funds (or 'rainy day' money) to cover six months worth of outgoings. If you had an illness or injury that kept you off work for a few months, or if you were made redundant, then six months might be a reasonable amount of time in which to get yourself sorted out. This is easier said than done however. For example, if your typical outgoings are £2,000 a month then you would need £12,000 in a savings account somewhere, which you never touch, just in case something goes wrong. If you can't manage this then PPI may be a suitable choice, particularly on high-value loans.

There is a lot of small print that you need to read before taking on PPI. For example, it will not cover you for a medical condition that you already have. Also, you will have to be in employment for a year before you can claim on the unemployment clause. If your PPI does pay out it will only normally be for 12–24 months after which you will need a source of income again.

There has been a lot of negative press regarding the mis-selling of PPI and also the insurance companies' unwillingness to pay out when claims are made. This has been investigated by the **Office of Fair Trading** and is ongoing. At the time of writing, 185,000 complaints of the mis-selling of PPI were being investigated by the Financial Ombudsman and an estimated two million people have been affected. If you think you have been mis-sold PPI then refer to www.financial-ombudsman.org.uk. If you *are* considering PPI then ultimately, this is a personal decision and depends on your financial circumstances and on your attitude to risk.

TEN IMPORTANT THINGS TO REMEMBER

1 *There are many different ways of borrowing money from hundreds of different organizations.*

2 *You should always shop around for the best finance deal, including switching providers if appropriate.*

3 *The APR is the best way of working out and comparing the cost of borrowing money.*

4 *There are often additional charges and penalty charges that apply when borrowing money.*

5 *You should always read the small print.*

6 *You should satisfy yourself that you can repay any credit agreement you choose to take on.*

7 *You should use your monthly budget plan to take account of all of your borrowing.*

8 *You can borrow money in the form of a loan, overdraft, credit card, store card, or credit agreement.*

9 *Debit cards and ATM cards are not a form of credit as you have to have sufficient funds in order to use them.*

10 *You should consider payment protection insurance whenever you borrow money.*

4

Savings and investments

In this chapter you will learn:
- *the principles of saving money*
- *what protection is available through the government protection scheme*
- *what rules of thumb you can apply when comparing savings products*
- *what the Annual Equivalent Rate (AER) is and how to use it*
- *what savings products are available including savings accounts, ISAs, bonds, shares, unit trusts and endowments*
- *whether you might want to consider ethical investments*
- *how to set up a pension and the different types available*

Introduction

Saving money is the simple act of putting some money aside for later. Usually this involves putting the money somewhere safe where it will increase in value, usually by earning interest. Effectively your savings are 'investments' as you hope that the value of your savings pot will grow over time.

There are lots of reasons why people save money and, in common with other aspects of financial services, there are hundreds of options.

The main factors you need to consider are:

- ▶ *What are you saving for?*
- ▶ *Do you need instant access to your savings?*
- ▶ *How long are you prepared to invest your money?*
- ▶ *How much risk are you willing to take with your savings/investments?*

There is always an element of risk when saving your money because the organization you choose to save with *could* lose it all! This is because when you save money, the bank or building society takes your money and invests it in other things, for example, in the stock market. Sometimes they make bad decisions and lose money. Sometimes they make good decisions and make lots of money. Most organizations are big and experienced enough to be able to make mostly the right decisions but banks, building societies and investment companies can and do get into trouble.

Insight

The Life Assurance business Equitable Life, which has been operating since the late eighteenth century and had 1.5 million investors, got into trouble in the late 1990s when they announced that they could not afford to pay the 'guaranteed bonuses' promised to investors. The court cases and enquiries have been running ever since with savers still waiting to get all their money back.

All UK savers are protected by the law up to a value of £50,000. This means that if your bank goes bust, the government will guarantee your savings up to this limit, per institution. If you are lucky enough to have more than £50,000 worth of savings you would be advised to split it between institutions to get maximum protection from this scheme. Note that this only covers money held in UK financial institutions so there is a greater element of risk if you choose to put your money in foreign banks.

There are some rules of thumb when it comes to saving. The first is that safer investments tend to attract a lower rate of interest.

For example, government Premium Bonds are one of the safest places to put your savings plus you have the chance of winning a large tax-free lump sum. However, on average the payout is much lower than the typical amount you would get from a savings account with a bank.

The second rule is that the longer you are prepared to tie up your money, the higher the interest rate you will get. This is because it gives the financial institution a longer period to invest your money before they have to pay it back.

The third rule is that the more money you invest/save, the better interest you will get on your savings. This is because the financial institutions are keen to get hold of as much money as possible so they can make more money from your money.

Annual Equivalent Rate (AER)

In the previous chapter we saw how important the APR was for working out how much it costs to borrow money. The **Annual Equivalent Rate** is the measure that you can use to work out how much money you will make when saving money. It shows the true value of how much interest you will earn over the year taking into account how often interest is paid and also factoring in the effect of any initial promotional rates.

There is another figure you will also see quoted on savings accounts and this is the '**Gross**' figure. This also refers to the amount of interest that will be paid on your savings. Sometimes the AER and Gross figure are the same and this is all to do with how often interest is paid.

In simple terms the AER is the amount of interest you would earn in one year. So if you saved £1,000 at 12% AER at the end of the year you would have £1,120. This assumes that interest is paid annually. If interest is paid monthly, then you will earn interest on your interest. So at the end of the first month 1% of interest is added, which means that the £1,000 is now worth £1,010. Next month, the interest is added to the £1,010 rather than the £1,000. If the interest rate stays the same for the year, you will make slightly more money by having the interest added on a monthly basis. The AER takes this into account whereas the Gross does not.

In practical terms it means that the Gross figure will be slightly lower than the AER figure. When comparing deals, make sure you use the same measure whether it be the Gross or the AER. Both are normally quoted anyway.

Savings accounts

A savings account is a bank account into which you pay lump sums or regular amounts. You can have a cash card and a cheque book on these accounts and you will be paid interest shown as an AER. The AER is closely related to the Bank of England Base Rate, which was explained in the Introduction. Many banks will offer deals that guarantee to track the Base Rate and stay above it. You will not be able to go overdrawn on these accounts.

Most bank and building society accounts normally come 'bundled' with a savings account. Often banks try to attract new customers by offering attractive savings rates. This has been the case during the credit crunch as banks have been keen to get hold of more money.

Most banks and building societies offer a range of savings products with their savings accounts falling into three categories: instant access, notice accounts and fixed rate accounts. **Instant access accounts** allow the most flexibility as you can get access to your money whenever you want it. However, they do tend to offer a lower AER than the **notice accounts** where you have to let the bank know in advance that you want to withdraw all or part of your money. The notice period could be anything from one month upwards with some attractive deals requiring a year's notice. You can often get your money out early but only subject to hefty penalties, which will massively reduce the AER in real terms. **Fixed rate accounts** offer a set AER over a fixed period, usually around a year. You cannot get access to your money in this time without heavy penalties.

The choice here depends on what your savings are for. If you are saving regularly for a major purchase, or simply saving to build up a nest-egg, then a Notice Account will offer better rates. However, if you need the flexibility, or want to move your money around to take advantage of better deals, then an Instant Saver would probably be preferable.

All accounts will have a minimum amount, which is usually £1. Higher AERs are sometimes on offer if you pay more in. As your savings grow, your bank should automatically move you onto a higher rate of interest if this is the case. Some savings accounts also have a maximum savings amount. Bear in mind that the government guarantee scheme will only cover £50,000 per institution, so you would be wise not to have any more than this with any one place anyway.

Comparison websites and almost all of the broadsheet newspapers publish 'best buy' tables so you can compare different savings products. There is some debate as to how impartial some of the comparison websites are and there is more on this in Chapter 10. Newspapers often collate their best buy tables from price comparison websites, so finding completely impartial advice can be difficult.

Also, as the deals change so often, what is a good deal one month, may be a bad deal the next month so you need to shop around and move your money to get the best rates (if you can be bothered). Many savings accounts now offer bonuses if you leave your money in for a set period. This is because the banks know full well that lots of us will move our money around following the deals, so they need to do what they can to hold onto us.

To make it easier to switch it is worth looking at the Internet-based accounts. An added advantage of these is that some of the 'e-saver' accounts offer slightly higher AERs as the bank's administrative costs are reduced because you never go into a branch or phone up their customer services people.

ISAs and bonds

In addition to the savings accounts, banks and other financial institutions offer other forms of savings products. These work in a similar way in that you put your money into them and they pay back interest based on the AER.

The **Individual Savings Account (ISA)** is a form of saving with tax benefits. They were introduced in 1999 to encourage more of us to save money. Normally when you save money you have to pay tax on any interest that you earn. This is because interest paid to you is classed as income and is therefore subject to **income tax**. The ISA allows you to save up to £5,100 in cash or £10,200 in shares each year without having to pay any tax on the interest you earn. If you do any form of saving, you should have an ISA to make the most of the tax breaks.

Insight

Ms A has a cash ISA and invests the full £5,100. The ISA pays 4% generating interest of £204 a year. As the ISA is tax free, she saves £40 a year in tax. Over the years these savings do add up and as interest rates increase, the tax savings will be even higher.

You set up an ISA in much the same way as any other account and there are lots of different providers to choose from including all the well-known banks. There are two types of ISA: the cash ISA and the stocks and shares ISA.

The **cash ISA**, as the name implies, is for cash savings only. It is basically the same as a savings account apart from the tax saving. You can pay money in and take money out and transfer balances from other ISA accounts, subject to a charge. The current tax-free limit is £5,100. Like savings accounts you can choose instant access, **fixed rate** and notice period accounts all of which offer different AERs. The same rules apply here as to normal savings accounts.

The **stocks and shares ISA** allows you to invest in selected stocks, shares and other bonds and funds approved by the government. The current tax-free limit is £10,200. The provider you choose here is critical as they will be playing the stock market with your savings. Therefore, the decisions you make about which provider to choose are critical and there is more on this in the investments section of this chapter.

As a general rule the cash ISA is a safer bet than the stocks and shares ISA, although the potential returns are lower. You can transfer your funds into a stocks and shares ISA at any time, but the rules will not allow you to transfer the other way round. If you do transfer between providers you need to make sure that your current provider treats it as a transfer and not an account closure, otherwise you may lose your tax breaks.

There is a range of **bonds** available both from the government and from the financial institutions. A bond reverses the traditional lender/borrower relationship in that if you buy a bond, it is the bank or government that owes you the money and they pay you back in the form of interest. So a bank might sell you £1,000 worth of bonds, which they then take and invest. In return they guarantee to pay you back your original amount plus interest shown as an AER.

There are hundreds of bonds that you can buy from the UK government, other countries' governments and a massive range from the financial services institutions. The thing to remember here is that it is you lending the money in this transaction so you have to satisfy yourself that the government or institution you are lending the money to, will pay you back. Therefore there is an element of risk, which can be minimized by avoiding the 'junk bonds' end of the market characterized by institutions you have never heard of offering AERs that are too good to be true.

UK government bonds are called **gilts** and are sold through a government department called the Debt Management Office (DMO): www.dmo.gov.uk. You can also buy through brokers. The amount of interest is often referred to as a 'yield' and the interest payable is called a 'coupon'.

The government also issue bonds and other savings through National Savings and Investments (NS&I): www.nsandi.com. This offers a range of products, some of which are tax free. The **Premium Bond** for example offers a guaranteed investment where you can buy between 100 and 30,000 £1 bonds. Each month your bonds are entered into a draw where they win prizes of anything between £25 and £1m. Your original investment is always safe and you can cash your bonds in at any time. You do not pay tax on anything you win.

This is a very complex market with the government and financial services institutions offering a range of other bonds all packaged up in different and usually confusing ways. The choice you make here depends on the usual factors of how much you want to invest, how long you want to tie up your money and how much risk you want to take. Just a few examples of the bonds on offer are shown below:

▶ **Fixed savings bonds:** *Usually have a minimum investment amount and require you to lock your money away for 12–24 months although they do offer a competitive AER.*
▶ **Index-linked bonds:** *Sometimes called equity bonds, these are usually linked to the performance of the stock market and guarantee that you cannot lose your original investment.*
▶ **Income bonds:** *These are designed to generate a monthly income from your savings without digging into the original amount invested.*
▶ **Children's bonds:** *Designed specifically for the under-18s these also have the advantage of being tax-free.*

Other investments

This section will take a whistle-stop tour of other ways of investing your money not covered in the previous sections.

Share trading is much easier now than it has ever been as you can become a trader from your own home via the Internet. In simple terms, if you buy shares you become a part-owner of the company and you have the right to attend their Annual General Meetings, vote, and take a dividend. The dividend is the amount per share that the company pay you for investing in them. Some investors take a long-term view with the companies they invest in and leave their money in for many years taking the dividend as an income. Other traders look for short-term gains and will sell their shares as soon as they have gone up in value. Obviously share trading is a massively complex business where you stand to make or lose lots of money. Information and tips on playing the stock market and not hard to find on the Internet. A good starting point is: www.moneysupermarket.com/shares/.

Unit and investment trusts are another way of investing in the stock market but rather than investing as an individual you put your investment into a trust that in turn makes investments. The advantage is that all investors' money is put into one pot where it is invested by experienced trust managers. Money can be invested in a range of ways including company shares, financial markets and property. There are varying degrees of risk associated with these and much of the success rests on the trust managers who tend to be the celebrities of the financial world. A good starting point is: http://www.whatinvestment.co.uk/.

Endowments are savings schemes with added insurance. You can buy an **endowment policy** from a bank or insurance company, paying a fixed monthly amount over several years, with the money being invested on your behalf. At the end of the period, you get back your original investment plus bonuses accrued from the success of the investment. In the past these were a very popular way of paying off a mortgage, as often there can be a lump sum left over at the end. However, they have declined in popularity as many policies did not make enough money even to cover the amount needed to pay off the mortgage. There have also been examples of mis-selling of endowment policies over the years where advisers have recommended them where they are not appropriate. One advantage is that they do have life insurance built into them and you can cash them in at any time. A good starting point is: www.thisismoney.co.uk. Here you can also find a link to information on what to do if you think you have been mis-sold an endowment policy.

Ethical investments have become increasingly popular in recent years as consumers become more aware of where their money is being invested. It means that your money will not be invested in any business or country that you think acts unethically. Typically this means not dealing with businesses who: deal with oppressive regimes; are involved in the arms trade; are involved in animal cruelty; have a bad environmental record. There is a FTSE4Good index (http://www.ftse.com/Indices/FTSE4Good_Index_Series/index.jsp) that identifies 47 businesses with recognized standards in social responsibility. Many investment trusts and pension schemes now offer ethical investments too.

Pensions

There is an old adage that states, 'if you think you understand pensions then you don't know enough about them', and this is because it is one of the most complex and fast-changing areas of personal finance. This is largely due to the fact that as a nation, in the future we will have a much higher percentage of people at pensionable age than we do now. Someone has to pay for this and it is likely to be us as individuals. We will all have to work until we are much older and rely more on our own efforts to provide a pension income.

In simple terms, a pension is a long-term savings scheme where you pay in regular amounts and if you are lucky, you will have an employer that also pays in regular amounts on your behalf. These amounts are tax-free but you cannot get your hands on any of the money until you retire. When you get to a certain age you should have a nice lump sum which you can cash in, taking some as cash and using the rest to provide an income for the rest of your days. This normally means buying an annuity which guarantees you a regular income.

On top of this you are still allowed to work while you are drawing your pension and if you are at the state retirement age and have paid all of your National Insurance contributions, you will also be eligible for your **state pension**. If your total income from state pension, private pension and work goes over the taxable limit, you will still have to pay income tax.

The idea is that by the time you retire, which can be at any age, you will have paid off your mortgage, got rid of any offspring and therefore have reduced outgoings. Consequently, you will not need the same level of income that you needed when you were younger. All of this depends of course on what kind of lifestyle you hope to have in retirement. The maths is quite scary as you can see from the example below. There is a simple rule here: the earlier you start the more you will have when you retire.

Insight

Mr D is a 40 year-old male paying in £250 a month from his £30,000 a year job. He hopes to retire at 65. Using a pension calculator he has worked out that this will only generate a pension income of £5,000 a year. He will need to pay in £1,000 a month to achieve a pension of £20,000. Many people plan a retirement income of two-thirds current salary, which would be unachievable for Mr D as he would not be able to afford his everyday expenses.

A good starting point to work out how much you are entitled to and how much you might need in retirement is http://www.thepensionservice.gov.uk/state-pension which includes a pension calculator to work out your entitlement. The Financial Services Authority (FSA) also provide a pension calculator to work out how much you would need to save into a private pension: http://www.moneymadeclear.fsa.gov.uk/tools/pension_calculator.html.

On top of the state pension you might have either a company pension scheme or a private pension. Some companies do not offer pension schemes as they are very expensive to operate, but may offer to pay into your private pension.

Company pensions usually require you to pay in a certain percentage of your salary which will be deducted monthly from your salary. The company will then add a percentage contribution on top, usually matching your investment. Company schemes therefore are usually the best option as twice as much goes into your pension pot. Also, all the administration is done by your payroll department saving you a great deal of time.

Many companies operate a 'final salary' pension scheme although these are becoming less common. It means that your pension income is calculated as a proportion of the salary you were earning just before you retired. More common now is the 'money purchase' scheme where the final pension pot is based on how much is paid in and how successfully this has been invested by the pension provider.

Private pensions are where you choose a pensions provider, usually one of the big insurance companies, and make monthly payments yourself. They invest your money and lots of other people's into stocks and shares and other investments via their 'pension fund'. Over the years you build up a pension pot, which you then cash in as soon as you think you can afford to live off what you have made. In essence these are just savings accounts, with the advantage that your contributions are tax free.

At the time of writing private pensions come in three main forms:

▶ **Personal pension:** *you choose the provider; you choose from a range of funds with different levels of risk attached and set up a monthly direct debit. When the fund is big enough you cash it in.*

- **Stakeholder pension:** *these are very similar to the personal pension except you can do this as an individual or you may also get contributions from your employer.*
- **Self-invested personal pension (SIPP):** *similar to the personal pension but rather than choosing a provider you select the individual businesses or funds that you want to invest your money in.*

Whichever you choose, the idea is to build up as big a pension pot as possible so that you can turn it into a regular income when you retire in the form of an annuity.

Annuities are a financial product where you pay a lump sum in return for a guaranteed ongoing income. In the UK you have to buy a retirement annuity by the age of 75. The idea therefore is that you take the lump sum that you have built up in your pension and buy an annuity. These are available from all the big insurance companies, which means that you need to shop around when the time comes to find the one that will offer you the best monthly income. Some annuities are linked to **inflation** via the retail price index (**index-linked**). This means that your annual income will stay the same in real terms, although you will get a lower monthly amount than a fixed annuity where the amount stays the same every year.

Choosing a pension provider for a private pension is very difficult. They will all claim to offer excellent returns over the long run and they will all charge you different amounts for operating your pension accounts in the form of an arrangement fee and an ongoing management charge, usually about 1%. The best advice is to try to balance out the company that charges you the lowest fees, with good performance going back over several years. This usually means you end up with one of the large well-known insurance companies. The FSA publish tables of charges and past performance at http://www.fsa.gov.uk/tables/. It may also be worth asking an **Independent Financial Adviser (IFA)**, some of whom specialize in pensions.

TEN IMPORTANT THINGS TO REMEMBER

1 *Saving is the process of putting money aside for later. Interest is paid on savings which means they will grow over time.*

2 *The Annual Equivalent Rate (AER) is used to measure the total amount of interest that will be paid on a savings account.*

3 *The AER will be higher if you save more money or commit your savings for longer periods.*

4 *Your savings are guaranteed by UK law up to £50,000 per institution, so if you are saving more than this, split it between institutions.*

5 *You need to shop around for the best deals and be prepared to switch as the deals change so often.*

6 *Individual Savings Accounts (ISAs) allow you to earn interest without having to pay tax on it, up to a certain limit.*

7 *You can increase the amount you get from your savings by investing in bonds, stocks and shares, investment trusts and other products. These tend to be higher risk but may also offer higher returns than traditional savings accounts.*

8 *You can get a higher AER if you are prepared to take higher risk investments.*

9 *Pensions are a form of long-term savings scheme, with tax-free contributions, which you cash in on retirement.*

10 *The earlier you start a pension scheme the better in terms of how much it is worth when it matures.*

5

....

Household expenses

In this chapter you will learn:

- *how the housing market fluctuates over time*
- *how mortgages work*
- *what types of mortgages are available and which might be the most suitable*
- *how to work out whether you can afford a mortgage*
- *how buildings and contents insurance work*
- *how to switch your utility suppliers to save money*
- *the ways in which you can get telecommunication services including phone, TV and Internet*

Introduction

For many households, the monthly mortgage payment represents the biggest single expense that they face. Add in other expenses directly related to owning and running a home, such as insurance, maintenance, utility bills and phone bills and many families will find well over half of their income disappearing before they even start spending money on things that are enjoyable.

Having said that, our homes usually represent the highest value **asset** that we own and over time the value of houses does tend to increase at a higher rate of inflation. So the ideal for many home owners is to pay off the mortgage during their working life. When the mortgage is paid, they can sell the house at a profit having enough money to buy somewhere smaller outright.

Historically, since the end of the Second World War, this has proved to be a safe bet. The graph below starts in 1947 and shows the year-on-year percentage increase in house prices over the years:

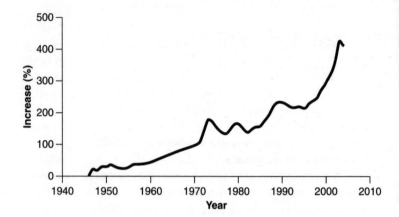

There are some peaks and troughs over time, but the overall trend is that house prices do increase. The worst scenario is 'negative equity' where your house is worth less than you paid for it. This is only a problem if you are trying to sell. If you sit tight then eventually the value of your house will increase. As a general rule, over a period of five years you would expect your house to be worth more than you paid for it.

For more background information and statistics about the housing market, try the Council of Mortgage Lenders at: http://www.cml.org.uk.

There is a culture of getting on the housing ladder as soon as possible in the UK. Around 70% of UK households are classed as owner-occupiers. Although there is an increasing number of people who now own their houses outright, the majority of us are paying a mortgage.

Mortgages

A mortgage is a long-term loan, typically over 25 years, used to buy property or land. The loan is secured against the property that you are buying, which gives the bank security if you fail to make your repayments. The total amount to repay is calculated, including the interest, and repayments are broken down into monthly amounts as with other forms of loan. This means that the bank actually owns the house until the final payment is made, at which point the deeds are sent to you and you can have a party.

The interest is shown as an APR in common with all of the other loans that we looked at in Chapter 3. As the loan is over such a long period, the compound effect means that in real terms the amount of interest you pay is quite high. For example, if you had a £100,000 mortgage over 25 years with an interest rate of 5%, you would have to pay back around £500 a month (depending on mortgage type), which would cost you around £150,000 over the period. This means that you are paying £150,000 for your £100,000 house.

There are different types of mortgage and we will look at each of them in this chapter. However, there are some basic principles for all mortgages, which are summarized here and explained in more detail below:

▶ *The amount of mortgage you are offered is based on your income.*
▶ *The amount of the mortgage will be less than the value of the house, typically up to 75% of the value.*
▶ *You will have to pay fees up-front to the lender, at the very least, for a property survey and valuation.*
▶ *Your repayments will go up or down based on the mortgage rate, which in turn is linked to the Bank of England Base Rate.*
▶ *You need to have insurance.*
▶ *You need to make your monthly repayments or risk repossession.*

The first basic principle is that the amount you can borrow is based on your ability to repay. The basic rule is that of the 'multiples', i.e. the lender will offer you a mortgage based on a **multiple** of your income. Typically, the bank will lend you three times your gross annual salary, or two and a half times your joint salary if you are getting a joint mortgage. This varies depending on who you get your mortgage from and you might find you can get a higher multiple than this. However, as with all loans, you and the lender need to satisfy yourselves that you will be able to make the repayments.

For example, if you earn £30,000, you will get a mortgage for £90,000, which won't buy you much in the current market. This is why throughout the 1990s and early 2000s, mortgage lenders were offering customers higher multiples so that they could afford to buy a house or flat. The problem with this is that the customers then struggled to afford the monthly repayments. Loans such as these that were being made to people who could not really afford the payments were known as 'sub-prime lending', where 'prime' refers to the people who could afford the repayments. Sub-prime lending was one of the factors that led to the credit crunch in 2008 where the banks and other lenders had so many loans that people could not afford to pay back. In these cases, the bank either had to repossess the home and try to sell it, usually for less than market value, or they had to renegotiate the debt and give the homeowner more time to pay.

The sensible way around this problem is to save up a deposit so that then you don't need such a large mortgage. For example, if you want to buy a flat for £120,000 and you earn £30,000, then you will need a deposit of £30,000 to add to your £90,000 mortgage. The issue here is that it will take you a long time to save up the deposit and you still need to live somewhere in the meantime, perhaps paying rent. This explains why so many people continue to live with their parents into their 20s.

Insight

Research carried out by GE Money indicates that the average age of the first-time buyer in the UK is now 34. The research also identifies that house price inflation over the last 30 years was 1436%. This means that if you bought a house for £2,000 in 1979, it would now be worth £287,200.

The second basic principle of the mortgage is what is called the '**loan to value**' or LTV. This is the amount of money that the mortgage lender is prepared to lend based on the value of the property. For example, many lenders operate a 75% LTV which means that they will only give you a mortgage that is 75% of the value of the house. For example, if the house you want is £100,000, they will only lend you £75,000. This is to cover themselves in case house prices crash. It means that house prices could drop by 25% and the house would still be worth more than the outstanding mortgage. If they have to repossess your house because you fail to make payments, they will still get their money back.

The third principle is that the amount you have to pay will vary depending on the mortgage rate. This is quoted as an APR and will vary depending on what is happening with the Base Rate. The Bank of England is in charge of the Base Rate and puts it up or down on a regular basis to try to encourage us either to spend more or save more. (Refer back to the Introduction for more details on this.) If the Base Rate goes up, your mortgage rate will go up, which means your monthly payments will go up. If the Base Rate goes down the reverse happens. At the time of writing Base Rates are at a historic low, which means that mortgages are relatively cheap. It also means that they are likely to go back up again over time.

The fourth principle is that you will have to pay some up-front fees to the lender. The amount of the fees depends on the type of mortgage that you get. In common with all financial services, the mortgage market is a very competitive one and banks and building societies are always trying to attract new customers. Therefore it pays to shop around to find the mortgage with the lowest APR and the lowest fees.

All lenders will insist on a **survey** to value the house. At your expense they send a surveyor round to check that the amount you are paying is appropriate for the house. This is because they will effectively own the house until the final payment so they want to make sure you are not paying too much. You can also pay extra to get a fuller report where the surveyor will carry out a much more detailed building survey checking for more serious problems such as structural issues or damp.

By law, all properties being sold are supposed to have a **Home Information Pack** or **HIP** (http://www.homeinformationpacks. gov.uk/). These may already contain information on the condition of the property so you might not want to pay again to have another survey.

The fifth principle is that you need to have buildings insurance and there is more on this in the next section.

The final key principle is that 'your home is at risk if you do not keep up the repayments' and this is worth some serious thought. In past years there has been a suggestion that the banks and building societies have been irresponsible in their lending. Most lenders now ask you to complete 'affordability sheets', which get you to think about all of your other spending as well as the impact of your mortgage. These are essentially budget plans so you may already have done one yourself. The government operates a 'mortgage rescue scheme' for people on low incomes and for those in negative equity. This aims to prevent people from becoming homeless. More details at: http://mortgagehelp.direct.gov.uk/index.html.

Finally, you need to factor in the **'stamp duty'**. This is a tax levied by the government on all house purchases over a certain amount. From 1 January 2010 the tax was set at:

- *House value between £125,000 and £250,001 = 1% stamp duty (e.g. £1,750 on a £175,000 house)*
- *Over £250,000 up to £500,000 = 3% stamp duty (e.g. £7,500 on a £250,000 house)*
- *Over £500,000 = 4% stamp duty (e.g. £20,000 on a £500,000 house).*

There are three key questions to ask yourself here:

1 *Can I afford the repayments now based on the current APR and on my income?*
2 *If interest rates go up can I still afford the repayments?*
3 *If I lose all or part of my income can I still afford the repayments?*

Question 1 is perhaps the easiest, although there is a case for taking a chance on extending yourself either to get your dream house, or to get a bargain house that you know you can add value to quite quickly.

Question 2 is a tricky one bearing in mind that at the time of writing, interest rates and mortgage rates are at record low levels. How would you cope if interest rates were 15% like they were 20 years ago, or even if they went up to 10%? The FSA have a mortgage calculator (www.moneymadeclear.fsa.gov.uk/tools/mortgage_calculator.html) that you can use to assess the impact of possible interest rate changes.

Question 3 is equally tricky and comes down to your attitude to risk. In Chapter 3 we looked at the concept of payment protection insurance and there are similar products available for mortgages. This type of insurance can be expensive and there can be lots of strings attached so it is one you need to look at carefully.

In terms of different types of mortgages, the market changes all the time and new mortgage products are invented. The main types at the time of writing are:

Repayment: the total amount borrowed and the interest over the period is all added up and then divided by the number of months you are going to have the mortgage for. You then repay this amount every month. Example: £100,000 mortgage over 25 years at 5% equals monthly payments of £550 for 300 months. The amount may go up and down if interest rates change.

Interest-only: the total amount of interest is calculated over the period of the mortgage and you only pay back monthly **instalments**

to cover the interest and not the amount borrowed. You will need to make a separate arrangement to pay off the original amount. This type of mortgage is popular because it reduces the monthly payment significantly compared to mortgages where you pay off the original amount and the interest borrowed. Using the example above you would save over £100 a month. However, you need to make alternative arrangements such as a savings account, ISA or an endowment to cover the lump sum at the end. The other plan would be to sell your house at the end and downsize leaving enough money to cover the original amount borrowed.

Flexible: usually a hybrid of one of the above that allows you to overpay or underpay your monthly amounts, pay in lump sums or even take a payment holiday. These might be suitable if you are self-employed or do not have regular income. They will also save you money if you think you will be able to overpay on a regular basis as this will reduce the amount of time you spend paying the mortgage and therefore reduce the total amount of interest you pay.

Tracker: these fix the mortgage rate to the Bank of England Base Rate so that you will always be paying interest that is around the same as the Base Rate. The advantage is that the lender is guaranteeing to pass on any reduction in the Base Rate direct to you. You will find that there are certain tie-ins and you will not be able to pay off the mortgage early.

Discount: these offer a discounted rate in the first couple of years and then move onto a higher rate later on. These are useful for first-time buyers who may be finding repayments difficult particularly as they have just bought their first home. If you are expecting your income to go up this may be a good way of getting onto the ladder but your longer term budget plans must allow for the increase when the discount period ends.

Fixed-rate: these fix the interest rate on the mortgage for a set number of years. Typically this is between one and five years. This gives peace of mind as it makes budgeting easier and if the Base Rate goes up it will not be passed on to you. However, if the Base

Rate goes down, you will not get the advantage of the lower rate. You will usually find that the APR is slightly higher than a normal mortgage. You also need to think about what happens when the fixed rate runs out as you may be faced with a sudden large increase in your monthly payments.

Offset: these are where you set up your savings interest to contribute to your mortgage payments. For example, if you have a mortgage of £100,000 and savings of £20,000, you can forgo the interest you would have made on the £20,000 but then only have to make mortgage interest repayments on the £80,000.

Buildings and contents insurance

The only insurance that your lender will insist on you having is **buildings insurance** which covers the entire structure of the home including garden buildings and walls. It also covers permanent fixtures such as kitchens and fitted wardrobes. You are covered against a range of threats such as subsidence, fire, flood and vandalism.

If you own your own house outright you do not have to have buildings insurance but if you are paying a mortgage, your mortgage provider will insist on you taking it out. Although they will provide you with insurance you do not have to take it out with the mortgage lender and you can shop around for a better deal. If you are a tenant you should not be paying for buildings insurance at all as it is not your house!

It is highly recommended to have buildings insurance even if you own your house outright as it is relatively inexpensive for what could be disastrous losses. Imagine if your whole house was gutted by fire and you had to rebuild from scratch. Buildings insurance is designed to cover the complete costs of a rebuild.

You can reduce the cost of buildings insurance by choosing to pay a higher **excess**. This is the amount that you have to pay yourself when you make a claim on an insurance policy. Also, you will find that it is cheaper to bundle the buildings insurance together with the contents insurance. You may also be offered introductory offers and no-claims discounts if you have never made a claim.

If your house is in an area that is prone to subsidence or flooding you may find that insurance companies may refuse to cover you, or may charge you higher premiums.

Contents insurance covers all of the other non-fixed items that are in your home. You can extend contents insurance to cover household items away from the home, e.g. electronic items, bicycles etc. Contents insurance is not compulsory and many people choose not to have it at all.

Insight

Mr B lives alone in a two-bedroom flat in a relatively crime-free area. For 20 years, Mr B has been paying an average of £150 a year for contents insurance. Therefore over the period he has paid £3,000 with nothing to show for it. He was burgled last year losing his wallet and a camera worth £150. As he had a £100 excess, he decided not to make a claim. Mr B continued to buy home insurance as he worked out that it would cost £20,000 to replace everything in his house if the worst did happen, e.g. a house fire.

You are insured against the usual range of risks including flooding, burst pipes, fire, theft and vandalism. You can pay extra and insure against accidental damage. This might be an option if you have young children or are particularly accident prone.

You can choose a 'new for old' policy which means that if you claim on your insurance you will get brand new items to replace what was damaged or stolen. This is more expensive than replacement or indemnity cover where the current value of the item is used. For example, if your five-year old TV gets damaged by water flooding from a burst pipe, you will be reimbursed for a five-year old TV, not a new one.

Some large-value items are not covered by standard insurance policies so you may need to list these separately and may have to pay additional premiums. For example, if you have expensive jewellery, or high value electronic equipment, it would be worth checking that the policy covers you. As a rule you should never assume that everything is covered – always check with the insurance company.

Utilities – gas, electricity and water

In the good/bad old days we used to have nationalized utilities and we all got our gas, water and electricity from our national or regional 'boards'. Since privatization we can now in theory shop around for the best deals for gas and electricity although it all still comes down the same pipes and cables. Large utility companies have now evolved where you can buy all of your utilities in one place, or even buy your electricity from the gas company!

Insight

Mr and Mrs L tried two switching websites (www.uswitch.co.uk and www.switchwithwhich.co.uk) to see if they could reduce their gas and electricity bills. They had to type in their postcode and some information on energy consumption from their last bill. The websites then suggested a range of alterative suppliers many of which were cheaper. They saved 10% by switching companies, which was easy to do. However, they are aware that the deals change quickly so although they have got the best deal now, that could change quite quickly.

The prices we pay for gas and electricity are extremely volatile with variations of up to 30% a year. It is relatively easy to switch gas and electricity suppliers although they all change their prices so often that it is difficult to keep up. There are also lots of tariffs to choose from to make the decision yet more difficult. You cannot switch your water supplier.

However, it is often worth the effort as there are savings of perhaps 20% to be made by switching suppliers, which could represent £200–£300 a year. The general advice would be to take a look at your utility bills perhaps once a year, or better still, after there has been a bit of a price war between the companies. For example, at the end of March 2009, six of the big suppliers cut their electricity prices by between 3% and 10%.

Many of the big suppliers will offer you extra discounts if you take your gas and electricity from them though you should not assume that this will be cheaper than shopping around for separate deals. You may be able to get a fixed or capped rate, which either fixes the price for a set period, usually a year, or guarantees that the price increase will not go over or below a set amount within a set period. These are popular and are worth looking at if you can get them. You usually have to act quite quickly as the deals do not last for long and go on a first-come first-served basis. Often the special deal is only available if you apply and manage your account over the Internet as this reduces the administration costs.

In summary, the best advice when looking at gas and electricity bills is:

▶ *Shop around continuously for the best deal and switch every time you think it is worth the time it takes you to do it.*
▶ *See if discounts are available for getting gas and electricity from the same provider.*
▶ *Use comparison websites to find the latest deals.*
▶ *Pay by direct debit and use an Internet account if you can as this often reduces the price. If you are on a pre-payment meter try to get off it as the best deals are usually on direct debit.*
▶ *Consider a fixed or capped rate if you can get one – but act quickly.*
▶ *Take regular meter readings as the man very rarely comes to read the meter these days and utility companies will use estimates.*

In terms of water suppliers you can't switch suppliers but you can switch to a water meter of you are not on one already. Depending on your water consumption you may be better off. This depends on the size of your house, how many people live in it and your lifestyle. The Water Consumer Council provide a 'water calculator' (http://www.ccwater.org.uk) to help you decide whether it is worth converting.

The final thing worth mentioning of course is that as energy prices seem to represent an increasingly large part of household expenses, we should all be looking at our energy consumption to see if we can reduce our bills that way. The philosophy here is that small changes in behaviour can lead to large savings. Energy savings products such as light bulbs and solar panels are becoming more mainstream and are now relatively inexpensive compared to the price we pay for energy.

Communications: landline phone, mobile phone, Internet, TV

There was a time when all telecommunications came through British Telecom but that has changed for many of us now. Many (particularly younger) people, have dispensed with the idea of a landline altogether and do everything through their mobile phones. The widespread growth of 'cable', particularly in urban areas means that many households now have a viable alternative to BT with phone, Internet and TV all coming down the same high-speed fibre-optic cables.

In rural areas the coverage of cable and even mobile telecommunications is much more variable as anyone who has ever been on holiday in North Devon will tell you. Having said that, even in the most rural areas, most households can now get reasonably good broadband access.

Much of this depends on who you have got in your household. If you have youngsters then you will be under great pressure to have as many channels as you can and the fastest telecommunications that you can get.

In terms of a landline phone, if you are not in a cable area then you will be paying for line rental and calls. Although these will be provided by BT, you can shop around to get fixed monthly rates where you pay another company, e.g. TalkTalk, and they then pay BT. The fixed deals include broadband Internet access and a certain number of calls usually split between peak and off-peak rates to other landline numbers. You can pay more to include calls to mobiles or international calls. If you do call overseas a lot type 'cheap international calls' into Google and choose from one of the many companies where you dial a number first and then get international calls for only a few pence per minute. An alternative is to use one of the VOIP services such as Skype which allows you to make calls to other Skype users free either over your phone, mobile or computer.

In terms of broadband Internet access, a good rule is only to pay for extra speed if you really think you need it. For example, half to 1Mb is sufficient if all you do is a bit of web surfing and emailing. If you or someone in your family wants to download lots of music or videos or play online games, then you might need the higher speeds advertised in Megabits (Mb). In theory the bigger the number of Mb, the faster your connection.

If you are in a cable area then typically you will enjoy faster broadband than households that get it down the telephone cables. You will also be able to get a bundled deal that includes telephone calls and cable TV stations. These usually represent good value compared to the cost of having these three services independently.

Mobile phones would warrant a whole book to themselves so there is only room for a few tips here. First, there are two main options which are 'pay as you go' and 'contract'. There are some very good contract deals around but bear in mind that they tend to tie you in for 18 months and getting out of them is not always straightforward. The simple rule is only to go onto contract if you are running up pay as you go phone bills that regularly go over the cost of a contract tariff.

Second, look for the SIM only deals that are becoming more popular. These are much cheaper than the standard phone deals and do not tie you into long contracts. With these you only pay for call time on the SIM card, which you can move from phone to phone.

Third, if you and several other members of your family all have mobiles and call each other a lot, then look at all going onto the same network as calls to the same network are significantly cheaper than calls to other networks.

Fourth is to look into the extras. Often mobile deals come bundled with a certain number of free calls and text but you may find that you are charged heavily for going over your limits, or for other services such as web access. The best advice here is to keep an eye on your monthly bill and adjust your tariff according to your usage.

TEN IMPORTANT THINGS TO REMEMBER

1 *The cost of buying and running your house probably represents your largest ongoing expense.*

2 *Historically, house prices always increase by more than the rate of inflation.*

3 *Mortgage rates are closely linked to the Bank of England Base Rate and will go up and down regularly.*

4 *A mortgage is a long-term loan used to buy property.*

5 *You should only take on a mortgage if you are satisfied that you can afford the payments now and in the future.*

6 *The amount of mortgage you can get depends on your income and the value of the property you want to buy.*

7 *There are several different types of mortgage to choose from.*

8 *You should take out buildings insurance and seriously consider contents insurance.*

9 *You need to shop around for the best deals on utility bills and be prepared to switch suppliers.*

10 *You need to shop around for the best deals on telecommunications and be prepared to switch suppliers.*

6

Insurance

In this chapter you will learn:
- *the basic principles of insurance*
- *to consider your own attitude towards risk*
- *how to find the best deal on any type of insurance*
- *the ways in which you can organize your car insurance*
- *what insurance options there are for insuring your health and getting access to health services*
- *what insurance options there are in case you are unable to work*
- *what insurance options there are to provide for your family in the event of your death*
- *what insurance options there are when travelling*
- *what specific insurance products exist for students living away from home*

Introduction

Insurance is where you pay money to an insurance company in the form of regular premiums and they promise to reimburse you in the event of loss. You can insure against almost anything. For example, David Beckham has insurance on his legs, Ant and Dec have insured each other's lives and Ken Dodd even insured his teeth. For the rest of us, we tend to insure things of value to us that would cost a lot of money to replace including our houses, cars and possessions. We also insure ourselves against injury or ill health as these could stop us from earning, or could lead to expensive medical treatment.

Insurance is all about risk. From our point of view we take a look at certain aspects of our lives and then look at how much it would cost us each month to insure against losing it. Some insurance is compulsory, for example car insurance, but most insurance becomes a matter of judgement.

From the insurance companies' point of view, it is all about probability and to be more specific, what is called 'actuarial analysis'. Insurance companies employ actuaries who, in simple terms, look at all of the money that they take in from premiums and then look at all of the money they pay out in insurance claims. A successful insurance company is one that pays out less than it takes in. In order to do this the actuaries mathematically assess the risk of everything by looking at different factors.

For example, if you are a 21-year old male looking to insure a fast sports car then your premium will be £3,000 plus. In fact, many insurance companies will refuse to insure you. This is because their statistics show that 21-year-old men in sports cars are much more likely to crash and therefore make a claim than other people. Conversely, if you are a 55-year-old woman driving a small hatchback your insurance would probably be less then £200.

All insurance operates on this basic principle. The more risky something is, the higher the insurance premium. So, often the decision you have to make is whether it is worth getting insurance at all, or you may simply be looking to reduce the amount of insurance premiums that you pay, while still covering yourself against major risks.

There are several other characteristics of all insurance types which are summarized here:

▶ *You pay a monthly amount called a premium. If you don't make a claim, you lose your premium. If you do make a claim, the insurance company will cover all or part of your loss.*

- *Insurance is generally renewed annually, at which time your new premium for the year is calculated.*
- *You can pay your premium as a lump sum or in monthly instalments. Insurance companies often charge more to pay monthly.*
- *If you don't make a claim on your insurance during the year, the premiums usually go down the next year. If you do make a claim, they normally go up.*
- *On most insurance there is an 'excess'. This is the amount that you have to pay if you make a claim.*
- *Insurance can be bought direct from an insurance company or through an insurance broker, who act as agents (salespeople) for the insurance companies in exchange for commission. Comparison websites act as agents.*

Attitudes to risk

Your attitude to insurance is largely down to your attitude to risk. Some people only take out insurance where it is compulsory and don't bother with anything else. Other people prefer to cover themselves for all eventualities. You can pay home contents insurance for years and never make a claim. Alternatively you might have a bad year where you get burgled, crash your car and have all your luggage stolen on holiday. Life is unpredictable.

Insight

These are genuine claims on car insurance policies at Norwich Union:

'A frozen squirrel fell out of a tree and crashed through the windscreen onto the passenger seat.'

'I couldn't brake because a potato was lodged behind the brake.'

'A herd of cows licked my car and caused damage to the paintwork.'

Given that insurance is all about probability it perhaps pays to be philosophical. For example, the chances are that if you go on holiday twice a year for 20 years, then eventually your luggage will get lost or stolen. There are two ways of looking at this:

▶ *It's worth taking out travel insurance every year as sooner or later I will need to claim on it.*
▶ *I'm willing to take the chance as it is unlikely to happen and when it does I'll just take the hit as it is probably cheaper than paying travel insurance premiums year after year.*

Another consideration is that insurance does bring peace of mind in that you know you are covered. With the holiday example, you can perhaps relax more knowing that you possessions are covered if the worst happens.

Many people choose insurance on a case by case basis and you can do this by looking at the costs and benefits. For example, not many of us take up the product protection insurance when we buy low-value electrical items. Insuring a £20 kettle for £10 does not make much sense as we would rather take the chance and just buy a new one when it breaks. On the other hand, paying £40 for multi-trip holiday insurance if we go away two or three times a year, or paying £5 a month for £100,000 worth of life insurance looks like a much better deal.

Before you buy any insurance it is worth checking that you are not already covered. For example, many businesses offer health insurance, PPI or death-only life insurance for their employees. Some credit cards and bank accounts include travel insurance. Some car insurance policies include breakdown insurance as standard. Check before you buy otherwise you will be paying twice for the same thing.

Car

Basic car insurance is compulsory by law. This is because you need to be insured against any damage you might cause to someone else or their vehicle if you crash into them. This is called '**third party**' insurance. An extension of this is '**third party, fire and theft**', which also insures your car if it gets stolen or if it sets on fire either accidently or through vandalism.

Third party or third party, fire and theft is usually the cheapest way of obtaining car insurance, though that is not to say it is cheap. In some cases, as a young driver you may be paying more for your insurance than your car is worth. The price of the insurance is calculated on a number of factors with the main ones being: age, motoring convictions, previous claims, type of car, size of engine and the number of miles you will drive each year.

Some insurance companies specialize in particular areas, for example, they only insure women drivers, or low-risk drivers who have not made any claims in the last few years. It pays to shop around for a quote, particularly if you are in the higher risk end of the market, i.e. you are young and male.

The other main type of car insurance is '**comprehensive insurance**' which also covers any loss you encounter through a claim, even if it is your fault. 'Fully comp' is generally not much more expensive than third party insurance so it is advisable to take this out. It has the added advantage of insuring you to drive other people's cars, though usually only on a third party basis.

With all insurance, your premium is adjusted every year and may go up or down. If you make a claim on your insurance during the year then the premium will go up, sometimes by a significant amount. Insurance companies offer quite large discounts for your '**no-claims bonus**', also called a **no-claims discount (NCD)**, which is the amount of years that you have been driving without making an insurance claim. You can pay an additional premium to protect your no-claims bonus. This means that even if you make a claim, your premiums will not go up the year after. This is not that expensive for experienced drivers.

Insight

Mrs R has been driving for 25 years. In that time she has never had to claim on her insurance so she has maximum no-claims bonus. It costs her around £200 a year to insure her Ford Focus. Last year she inadvertently left the handbrake off when parking the car and it rolled into another vehicle causing £500 worth of damage. Mrs R had insured her no-claims bonus so her insurance company settled the claim and her insurance premium stayed the same the following year.

All the major insurance companies offer car insurance and there are hundreds of specialist car insurance companies and brokers to choose from. It can be cheaper going direct to the insurance company but this is not always the case. The start point is to get a quote, which you do by phoning or filling in an online form. This is actually quite time-consuming as they ask for a lot of information, but your insurance is only valid if you give them it and it is accurate. If you do have to make a claim and the insurance company finds that you have given them false information, then they will not pay the claim, leaving you with a large bill.

There is also protection available if you get hit by an un-insured driver. Many insurance companies are now offering this as standard. There are large numbers of un-insured drivers on the road, as many as one in 20 according to the RAC. The fact that they don't have insurance is usually because they can't afford it so you will probably be unable to recover any money even if you pursued them through the courts. Therefore, it is worth doing what you can to protect against this.

This area of insurance is one where the comparison websites are really useful as you only need to fill in one form and they then go off and do the searching for you. These sites will often find the best deal quite quickly but in exchange you may find yourself getting unsolicited phone calls and emails from the insurance companies listed on the website.

Health/medical

In this section we will be making a distinction between private health insurance, also called private medical insurance, and health plans. Private health insurance covers you against the cost of medical care in a private hospital, or in a private ward in an NHS hospital. Health plans cover you for more routine trips to the dentist, optician or other medical specialists. The line between the two can get blurred and many health insurance companies will offer a combination of both.

Private **health insurance** was once seen as the domain of the very wealthy although it is becoming more affordable now. In common with the nature of all insurance, the premiums will be more expensive if you are in higher risk categories. Typically, people who smoke, are obese or have a history of high blood pressure or high cholesterol will pay higher premiums. Also, as you get older you can expect your premiums to increase.

You can choose plans that cover individuals, couples and families, which entitle all named individuals to private treatment in a hospital of their choice without having to wait on an NHS waiting list. Most major illness groups are covered by the insurance and this includes in- and out-patient treatment.

Health insurance is one of those areas where you really do need to read the small-print. In particular you need to check what exclusions apply to the policy. These are the things that the policy does not cover. Sometimes aspects are not covered that you might assume would be. For example, some policies will not cover you if your health issues are as a result of an occupation that is not your main occupation. Also, you should check where you can receive treatment as some policies do not allow you to choose your own hospital.

Health plans tend to be for the more predictable aspects of health care such as regular check-ups with your dentist or optician.

Most of these operate on a cash-back system where you send in a claim form after a visit and receive a standard amount depending on the treatment. The amount they pay is set and is not usually based on your age and if you claim, it does not normally affect your premium next year. As the amount you can get for each treatment is fixed, this insurance tends to be much cheaper than private health insurance.

Insight

Mrs B pays £3.45 per week into a Health Plan. The main features of the plan are that she can have dental check-ups and treatment and eye tests and treatment up to the value of £200 a year. She is also covered for chiropody, osteopathy and physiotherapy up to a value of £300 of treatment.

Accident, sickness, redundancy and critical illness cover

The key principle of **accident, sickness and redundancy** insurance is that you are insuring yourself for loss of earnings in the short term (usually for one year) if you find yourself unable to work through no fault of your own. A variation on this is 'income protection insurance' which covers longer-term conditions that leave you unable to work for periods of longer than a year.

Accident, sickness and redundancy policies are extendable in that you can pay extra premiums to cover yourself for disability or unemployment. You may find that there are quite a few strings attached, for example, you will not be able to get cover on pre-existing medical conditions. There has been some debate as to whether or not it represents good value for money.

The basic features of this insurance are that you will pay a monthly premium based on your age, occupation and medical history. In the event of illness, accident or unemployment the policy will pay out regular monthly amounts designed to cover your living expenses until you are able to get back to work.

There is usually a cap on the total amount that these policies will pay out, typically about half of your gross annual salary. Therefore you can expect the policy to cover you for around six months before you have to find another source of income. As with payment protection insurance, you might think that a better bet would be to try to build up some **rainy day money** to cover this eventuality.

The key principle of **critical illness insurance** is that you are providing yourself with a lump sum in the event of being diagnosed with certain illnesses. The lump sum can be used for anything. For example, you could use it for palliative treatment, or to make adjustments to your home, or to go on holiday.

The 'selling point' of these policies is that critical illnesses will probably leave you unable to work although they won't actually kill you, so having a lump sum will give you one less thing to worry about.

Life Insurance and Family Income Benefit

Life insurance is quite straightforward (and a prime motivation for murder in all good detective books!). Confusingly it is also sometimes called life assurance. You pay a monthly premium and in the event of your death, a lump sum is paid to your next of kin. There are no other benefits to the insurance and they are often referred to simply as 'death-only policies' although some also pay out for terminal illness. You can take out an individual policy, or a joint policy, usually with your partner, which typically pays out on the first death.

The main question when taking one of these out is whether you need to leave anyone a lump sum. It makes good sense for parents to have individual life policies on each of their lives, as the lump sum can be passed to the spouse or down to the children. You might also use a life policy to cover any debts that would be left on your death. However, many people carry on paying for life insurance even though there is no real need for a lump sum on their death. For example, most mortgages have death cover so they would be cleared anyway.

Death-only policies are relatively inexpensive particularly for young people. For example, a 25-year old male can pay just £5 a month and insure his life for £100,000. As you get older the premiums get higher for the same level of payout. Other personal factors are taken into account such as your medical history and whether or not you smoke. As with all forms of insurance, the higher the risk the higher the premium.

There are two main types of life insurance: level term and decreasing (also known as mortgage) cover. **Level term** means that the lump sum amount is fixed and will be payable if you die at any point during the plan. Typically a plan might last for five or ten years, after which the insurance company will want to re-calculate your premiums as quite frankly, you are closer to dying. A **decreasing insurance policy** means that the lump sum assured goes down every year. These are often used to protect a mortgage where the amount needed goes down each year as it is being paid off.

A variation on the death-only policy is the **Family Income Benefit** plan, which rather than providing a lump sum, provides a regular monthly amount on the event of your death for a fixed period of time. This might be particularly suitable if you have children and want the peace of mind of knowing that you are leaving an income. You may choose to have one of these and a death-only policy so that you are also leaving a lump sum.

The basic principle is that you choose the period over which you want the plan to run. For example, you might start one when your child is born that then runs for 18 years. You then choose how much you want the monthly premium to be and this is calculated to see what that would return in terms of a monthly amount in the event of your death. The plan lasts for the time stated which means you have to pay in for 18 years to keep up the policy. If you die, it will pay out until it expires.

Travel

Travel insurance covers you against a range of losses that might happen when you are away as well as costs that you may incur if something goes wrong. Typical travel insurance covers aspects such as loss of baggage, costs incurred if there is a travel problem and cover relating to health. Travel insurance is usually available for a single trip or for multiple trips taken in one year. Obviously single trip insurance is cheaper but if you know you are going away more than once it is probably worth buying a multi-trip policy.

Premiums are usually paid as a lump sum rather than instalments as travel insurance is relatively cheap compared to other forms of insurance. For example, a 40-year-old single woman travelling through Europe would probably pay around £20 a year for multi-trip insurance.

Premiums do vary depending on where you go, how many people you are insuring in your party and what you are doing. For example, if you are doing anything risky you will find it more expensive. There are some specialized areas of travel insurance and these include things such as winter sports and back-packing where you can expect to pay higher premiums. If you are travelling as a family you can get cover for the whole family and often the children are covered for free. There is also specialized cover for older travellers.

In return for your premium the typical travel policy covers: death expenses including repatriation; medical expenses; personal possessions and cash; cancellation or curtailment; personal liability if you injure someone else. In each case there will be a maximum amount payable.

It is worth checking your travel insurance for what is *not* covered and these will be listed as policy exclusions. For example, if you miss your flight because you didn't leave enough time to get to the airport then you are not covered. With some budget airlines you will not be covered for delayed or cancelled flights. You also need to check that the country you are travelling to is covered and that the specific activity you are taking part in is also covered. For example, some standard policies do not cover you on a cruise.

In addition to all the big insurance companies there are many small specialized holiday insurance companies that you will find listed in the back of the travel section of newspapers, on Teletext or on the Internet and price comparison websites. As with all financial services it is worth shopping around.

Students

Students warrant a special (albeit brief) mention here as it is often assumed that when they go off to university all of their possessions are covered under the contents insurance policy of the family home and this is usually not the case. In some cases universities will offer basic contents insurance to students living in their halls of residence.

Often students will have a small number of high value items such as laptops, mobile phones, bicycles and stereo equipment.

Consequently many insurance companies do offer specific student insurance policies to cover these items in addition to standard contents insurance described in Chapter 5.

Another peculiarity of being a student is that you are likely to live in shared accommodation with communal areas. Specialized students insurance will cover against theft and vandalism from 'walk-in' crimes so it is not necessary for a break-in to take place before the policy pays out. Possessions are usually covered while in transit to and from university and even in the family home during holidays.

Pets

Finally in this section is the fairly recent innovation of **pet insurance**. Essentially this is like the health plans discussed earlier in this chapter, but for your pets. Given the cost of vet's bills, these have become increasingly popular in recent years.

In addition to covering sickness, illness or accident you can also cover yourself against any claims made against your pet if it injures someone or another animal, any cancellation fees from holidays because your pet is ill, and even cover against paying a reward if your animal gets kidnapped.

As with all insurance policies there are certain exemptions and some types of dogs are not covered. You cannot insure against pre-existing medical conditions and certain medical procedures are not covered.

Pet cover is relatively inexpensive. For example, annual cover for a three-year-old cross-breed would cost less than £10 a month offering up to £40,000 worth of cover. This would cover you for most vets' bills in the case of illnesses and accidents. Most standard insurance companies deal with cats and dogs but you will need a more specialized insurer for larger and more unusual animals. Premiums are likely to be much higher reflecting the higher cost of treating such animals.

TEN IMPORTANT THINGS TO REMEMBER

1 *Insurance is all about probability. We pay small amounts now to protect against big losses later.*

2 *The higher the risk involved, the more expensive insurance becomes.*

3 *Your attitude to insurance depends on your attitude to risk.*

4 *You should consider all forms of insurance although some are better value for money than others.*

5 *You need to shop around every year for the best insurance deals.*

6 *Basic car insurance is compulsory. All other forms of insurance are optional.*

7 *You can insure almost anything but most people insure their car, house, possessions, life, health and pets.*

8 *There is a range of insurance covering loss of earnings through sickness, illness or unemployment.*

9 *If you have dependants then health and life insurance are more important.*

10 *Specialized insurers are worth considering if you have specific requirements.*

7

Banking

In this chapter you will learn:

- *the basic principles of banking*
- *the ways in which you can manage your bank account either online, over the phone or in the branch*
- *the different types of bank account available and which might be the most suitable for you*
- *how to open a bank account*
- *how to understand a bank statement*
- *how to switch banks*
- *what bank charges you might incur for banking services*
- *how direct debits and standing orders work*
- *what to do if you have a problem or complaint*

Introduction

The banking world has taken a bit of a battering over the last few years. Rewind a generation and the bank manager used to be a bit like the family doctor. He or she got to know you and your family well and made decisions that were in the best interests of you and the bank. If you wanted a mortgage you had to put on your best clothes and go and ask nicely for the money.

Nowadays, most of us don't know our bank manager and our local branches may not even have one. An increasing number of us bank online now and never even go into a branch. We are far more likely to deal with call centre staff or branch customer advisers who are following a rule book when it comes to the way they deal with us. Decisions about lending are largely guided by computerized **credit-scoring** systems rather than personal decisions.

In recent years many banks have got into trouble because of the way that they lend money and trade in debts. However, before we get too sentimental about the old days, modern banking is much better in many ways. We now have 24-hour access to our money from ATMs all over the world, the banks themselves are open longer, **online banking** is convenient and available all the time and all of these services can be accessed for free.

We need banks as they provide us with:

- *somewhere safe to keep our money*
- *convenient methods of paying for things*
- *interest on our money.*

Banks need us as we provide them with:

- *cash deposits that they can invest to make yet more money*
- *interest payments on borrowing*
- *payments for services.*

The way that most banks work is that you will go to them for a particular reason, for example a loan with a low APR or a savings account with a high AER. Once you have bought one financial product from them, they are able to offer you a range of other products and services.

This can be very good for the customer as the banks are always competing against each other to get new customers and will offer attractive deals. The downside is that the deals are constantly changing so if you switch to a good deal one month, it may be superseded by a better deal somewhere else next month. Obviously you can switch banks and there is more on this later in this chapter.

Bank accounts: current, savings, premium, online, telephone

The **current account** is the 'bread and butter' account for most banks. This is the main account that you will use for everyday spending. Typically, the bank will require you to pay a certain amount in every month, usually your wages. In return you get access to your money via ATMs, a cheque book and a debit card. Some banks will also offer interest on the money you have in your bank if you are in credit or other incentives to encourage you to open an account. If you take out a loan with a bank, they normally insist that you have a current account with them.

For most of us, our current account is very fluid in that there is money going into it on a regular basis and money going out of it all the time. Many people keep a close eye on the balance of their current account either online or through an **ATM** and make sure that the amount they spend each month does not exceed their balance. A significant number of people operate an overdraft to take account of small over-spends at the end of each month prior to their wages being paid in. Many banks will offer free overdrafts up to a certain limit as standard.

You can operate a current account either through a branch, online or over the phone. You need your magic numbers for all of this which are typically:

- ▶ *your **PIN** for the ATM (a four-digit number)*
- ▶ *the bank **sort code** (a six-digit number)*
- ▶ *the bank **account number** (usually a nine-digit number)*
- ▶ *the debit card number (a 16-digit number).*

If you know all of these off by heart, you probably spend too much money! On a more serious note, armed with these numbers, anyone can clear out your bank account so you need to protect them.

Most current accounts are free to operate, which actually is a pretty good deal. The bank keeps your money safe and lets you have it whenever you want it in a variety of convenient ways and doesn't charge you a penny for this service.

Some banks offer **premium current accounts** which offer additional services and benefits for a monthly fee. Typically you might pay a £10 per month service charge to have one of these accounts and in return you might get a larger free overdraft limit, discounted insurance, breakdown cover and preferential rates on other services such as hotel stays. Sometimes these are not very good deals. The way to look at these is to work out what they will cost you over the year and then look at the cost of benefits you receive and think carefully about whether you are actually going to use them.

Insight

Mrs A chose to pay £12 a month for an enhanced current account as it came with free breakdown cover for her car among other benefits. This is £144 per year. At the end of the year she realized that the only feature of the account she had used was the breakdown cover. When she renewed her car insurance she was offered discounted breakdown cover at £60 per year. Consequently the current account was not a particularly good deal.

We have already looked in detail at savings accounts in Chapter 4, but it is worth mentioning here that banks often offer attractive savings rates on savings accounts linked to their current account. This is one of the main ways that banks attract new customers.

Many accounts are now only available as online or telephone accounts. Over recent years many banks have been closing branches, partly to save money and partly because not so many of us use branches any more. This reduces their overheads significantly. As a consequence they are sometimes able to offer better deals to customers who take up online-only or telephone-only accounts.

Telephone banking has been around for several years now. At one time it operated under the cosy title of 'armchair banking'. This has been taken over now by online or Internet banking. You can still phone a human if you need to, but the idea is that we do most of it ourselves. All you need is a computer, Internet access and basic computer skills. You can do almost everything online that you would normally do in a branch, such as:

▶ *check your balance*
▶ *pay bills*
▶ *set up direct debits and standing orders*
▶ *transfer money between accounts.*

The one thing you can't do is physically pay in cash or cheques. To pay in cash you need to go into a branch or use an ATM. To pay in cheques you either need to go into a branch, post them with a paying in slip or use an ATM. An increasing number of transactions are now being made electronically which means that cash and cheques never need to change hands. In fact we may have to explain to the next generation what a cheque was!

It is worth mentioning the issue of online fraud and **identity theft** here. According to the Office of Fair Trading (www.getsafeonline.org/) nearly a quarter of us have been or know someone who has been the victim of an online fraud of some sort. The most common in terms of online banking is the '**phishing** attack' where you are sent an email supposedly from your bank asking you to verify your sort code and bank account number. The email will link you to a very realistic website that will have a web address that is very similar to a real bank. These can be very convincing but there is a simple rule. No bank will ever email you and ask you for your banks details so if you get an email like this, it is a phishing attack. Delete the email without opening it and, if you feel inclined, you could inform the bank.

Opening and operating a bank account

Opening a bank account is relatively easy. You can do it in a branch, by post, over the phone or online. Basically you fill in a big form.

You will need to provide the bank with personal financial information relating to your income and your outgoings, including borrowing. They may require written proof of identity and earnings.

Within a few days you will receive your cards and cheque book and all of the numbers you need to operate the account a day or so later. The bank doesn't send them in the same envelope for security reasons. You will need to make an initial deposit into the account and inform your new employer of the sort code and bank account number so that they can pay your wages automatically into the account each month.

You should keep a regular eye on your account. You can do this by looking at your **bank statement**. This is a record of all the money going in (credits) and out (debits) of your account. If you bank online you can view these whenever you like. Alternatively, you can get mini-statements out of an ATM that will show your last few transactions, or you will get a full statement each month. You can also telephone or go into your bank, and ask for a balance.

An example statement is shown opposite with each of the main parts explained. Different banks have different layouts but the same basic information will be shown regardless of who you bank with.

The main parts of the statement are:

The name, address, account name and numbers details: to verify that it is the right account.

Date of statement: statements are normally sent out each month and will be made up of a number of pages depending on how many transactions need to be listed.

Opening balance: this is the amount in your account at the beginning of the first day over the period that this statement covers.

A Bank
Phone 08450 000 000
www.abnk.co.uk

Mr and Mrs A
1 Acacia Avanue
Anytown
Hereshire HE1 1AA

Current Account

Account name: Mr and Mrs A	Sort Code: 00-00-00	Account number: 123456789

Statement date: 31/03/09
Page 1 of 4

Opening balance: £1245.34 OD
Money in: £2453.00
Money out: £1435.00
Closing balance: £227.34

Overdraft limit: £2,000

Date	Description	Money Out	Money In	Balance
BROUGHT FORWARD			1245.34 OD	
01 March	NSPCC		50.00	1295.34 OD
01 March	Mortgage Co. Ltd		750.00	2045.34 OD
02 March	TFR000011111	2453.00		407.66
02 March	Gas		50.00	457.66
03 March	203456		75.00	532.66
04 March	203457		15.00	547.66

Money in and Money out: these are useful as they show the totals for the period of the statement. This means you can see at a glance whether you have spent more than you earned.

Closing balance: this is the amount left in your account on the last day of the statement period. It becomes the opening balance of next month's statement.

Overdraft limit: this shows how much your **authorized overdraft** limit is if you have one.

Transactions: the main body of the statement is each individual transaction that has taken place over the statement period. It shows the Money in (sometimes labelled as credit) and Money out (sometimes labelled as debit). The Balance is a cumulative total which shows the amount left in your account after each transaction. Notice that if you are overdrawn it is shown as OD. The Description column helps you to identify what the transaction was although it is not always easy to tell. Often this will contain the name of the company that you paid money to, or a cheque number or some indication that it was an ATM transaction.

The main reason to keep an eye on your account is for budgeting reasons. Most of us tend to underestimate the amount we spend. The consequence of this is that you may go over your overdraft limit, which means you will get charged, potentially for every day you stay over the limit. If you do go overdrawn, inform the bank as soon as possible as an authorized overdraft is significantly cheaper than an **unauthorized overdraft**. If you are on a tight budget, regular monitoring of your account is even more important. With online banking, you can do this as often as you like.

Mistakes do happen, for example, money being taken out twice, or you may be a victim of fraud. If someone gets hold of your numbers and starts taking money out of your account, the sooner you notice this the better. If your cards get lost or stolen or you notice irregular amounts leaving your account you should inform the bank immediately and they will put an instant stop on any money coming out of the account. You will then have to wait a few days until a new set of cards and numbers are sent.

You also need to be aware of what banks call **clearing**. This is the amount of time it takes for money to be moved from one account to another. Clearing can take anything from a few minutes to five days. For example, if you transfer money electronically from your current account to your savings account with the same bank, then that is an instant transaction. An electronic transaction to a savings account held with a different bank can take anything from a few hours to a few days. When you pay in a cheque, it will typically take three days to clear. You do have to take this into account when you are budgeting. On your bank statement you will see cleared and **uncleared items**. **Cleared items** are those transactions which are completed and uncleared are those where the money is not actually in the bank yet.

Switching

Many people have a bank account opened for them as a child and then stick with the same bank for years. However, more and more people choose to switch accounts now, incentivized by higher interest rates on credit balances, or other offers. The process of switching is relatively straightforward as it simply means filling in another form. Although you do not necessarily have to close your existing account in order to switch it is advisable to do so to avoid any charges that may go on your dormant account, and to prevent it being used fraudulently. Bank accounts can be closed over the phone or in writing and you will be asked to destroy or return your cards and cheques.

The comparison websites all include current accounts and the banks are continually advertising the latest deals. In fact, it's almost impossible to avoid being sold a new current account from one week to the next.

However, the problem is that there are so many things linked to your current account that it can often take a month or two to get the new account fully operational. For example, the payment of your wages and all of your direct debits and standing orders will be linked to your current bank. You need to ensure that you swap them all to the new account or you may find that your gas bill is not being paid. Some banks do offer to take care of all of this for you although you may feel more confident if you did it yourself.

Insight

Mr and Mrs H changed bank accounts after 15 years with the same bank. They printed out a list of all direct debits and standing orders and re-instated all of them with the new bank. Their local council rejected the new standing order for the first two months as their automated system did not recognize the new details. As a consequence Mr and Mrs H received a summons for non-payment of council tax including an additional £40 added for administration costs. The council argued that it was Mr and Mrs H's responsibility to ensure that the money was paid each month.

Account charges

Most current accounts offer basic banking for free. It is possible to avoid any charges on the account (**account charges**) if you keep it in credit (or within the agreed overdraft limit) and stick to all of the rules. You will incur charges if you request particular services, if you exceed your overdraft limit or if you choose one of the premium accounts mentioned earlier.

Banks do charge for some services, for example, cancelling a cheque, ordering extra statements and exchanging currency and these charges are levied as one-off payments when you use the service. Typical charges are shown in the table below although these do vary from bank to bank.

Service	Charge
Overdraft Usage Fee	50p a day for no more than ten days in each monthly charging period (up to £5)
Exceeding Overdraft Limit Fee	£5 a day for no more than 20 days in each monthly charging period
Stopping a payment	£10
Banker's Draft	£10
Paper copy of a statement	£5
Card transactions abroad	3% of transaction
Cash withdrawal abroad	2% for advancing cash + 3% of transaction

Most banks will charge you for:

▶ *exceeding your overdraft limit – even if only by £1 you can typically be charged £25 for every day you stay overdrawn*
▶ *'bouncing' a cheque – where there is not enough money in the account to cover the cheque; this is a one-off charge of as much as £40*
▶ *'bouncing' a direct debit – where there is not enough money in the account to pay it; this is a one-off charge of as much as £40.*

This has been a hot topic over recent years with the banks being heavily criticized by customers and consumer groups for overcharging, particularly customers who can least afford it. This is a controversial issue. The banks would argue that their charges are very clearly stated and that there are clear rules. If you stick to the rules you don't have to pay anything to operate most current accounts. The only way they can afford to offer free banking is by charging those people who do not stick to the rules. Consequently, customers who regularly exceed their overdraft limits will pay charges so that those who don't can enjoy free banking.

Many customers are trying to sue the banks for what they see as over-charging and this has been running through the courts for a couple of years now. Some customers have won some of their charges back but the banks are fighting the cases strongly. The best advice is:

▸ *Avoid this situation by keeping a close eye on your bank statements and the balance of your account so that you have enough to cover your cheques and direct debits.*
▸ *If you do think you need to go overdrawn, contact your bank immediately and make sure your overdraft is authorized. You will still pay interest on the overdraft but will avoid the charges.*
▸ *It is possible to reclaim charges from the bank if they are excessive. This is a grey area at the time of writing as test cases are still running through the courts. More information is available from the Financial Ombudsman (www.financial-ombudsman.org.uk) or the FSA (www.fsa.gov.uk).*

Insight

Mr H was charged £35 every time a payment was made which was over his overdraft limit. This happened three times on one day when three transactions – a cash withdrawal, a cheque and a debit card payment – all went out on the same day. This meant that in one day he was hit with charges for £105, all for going a few pounds over his overdraft limit.

Direct debits and standing orders

A **direct debit** is an instruction that we give to our bank to make a regular payment into another bank account. The nature of direct debits is that they are for payments that we know we need to make every month, typically for mortgages, gas, water, electricity, credit cards and insurance. We may also have direct debits for more interesting things such as subscriptions to magazines and club memberships.

We have to authorize the direct debit payment, which can be done over the phone or via a direct debit mandate which is a simple form that requires our sort code, bank account number, signature, amount and payment date. Once set up the other bank account, e.g. the gas company's bank, will request the amount each month on the stated date and this will run until you cancel it.

The amount paid using a direct debit can change but they must let you know in advance if they are going to change the amount. For example, many of us pay our gas bills by direct debit but the price of gas can vary significantly over the year. If the price of gas goes up then our direct debit payments need to go up to cover it. Conversely, if the price of gas goes down we end up in credit on our gas bills. The gas company normally reviews the monthly amount on an annual basis, or when the prices go up.

There are some reported problems with direct debits mainly to do with companies changing the direct debit amount without informing customers, or even setting up direct debits incorrectly. The problem can be compounded if the incorrect payments push you overdrawn and you then incur bank charges. Problems do happen but given that there are millions of direct debit transactions taking place every day, the system is quite robust. In common with other areas of banking the best advice is to keep a regular eye on all the payments that are going out of your account to check they are correct. If you suspect any errors, contact the bank immediately.

A **standing order** is similar to a direct debit in that it is an instruction we give to the bank to make a regular payment to someone else. The difference with the standing order is that it is for a fixed period and it is the customer who sets it up and is the only one who can change the amount. Standing orders are normally used for payments where the monthly amount is unlikely to vary such as council tax, rent or possibly your mortgage.

Many companies will not accept standing orders as a payment method but instead insist on a direct debit as they want to have control over the monthly amount. Although we have more control over a standing order we also have the responsibility of making sure that it is paid (see the Insight box on page 110). If there is some problem with the payment, it could mean that critical bills do not get paid.

Regulation and complaints

At the time of writing the UK banks are regulated by the
Financial Services Authority (FSA), which reports directly to
the government. There is much debate about how effective they
have been in light of the banking crisis and the credit crunch
that hit in 2008. The suggestion is that banking **regulations** may
be much stricter from now on as many of the banks failed
and had to be taken over by other banks or bailed out by the
taxpayer.

Many of the banking regulations exist to control how the banks
deal with each other. There are also regulations and codes that
protect us as customers. All institutions that offer savings and
investments must be authorized by the FSA, although other aspects
of finance including general banking tend to operate under a
voluntary scheme.

The main areas of customer protection and information are:

▶ *The government protection scheme called the* **Financial
  Services Compensation Scheme (FSCS)** *guarantees to repay
  up to £50,000 of our money (per institution) if that institution
  fails (http://www.fscs.org.uk/).*
▶ *The* **Banking Code Standards Board** *(http://www.
  bankingcode.org.uk) is made up of most of the major banks
  and building societies in the UK working closely with the FSA
  and the Office of Fair Trading (OFT). The Banking Code
  is a voluntary code defining the way that banks should deal
  with their customers and this board monitors and intervenes
  where there are breaches. The full document can be accessed
  from this website and covers all aspects of banking including
  charges, interest rates and the way that financial services are
  advertised.*
▶ *The* **Financial Ombudsman Service** *(http://www.
  financial-ombudsman.org.uk/) is an independent organization
  set up by parliament who you can go to with complaints about*

any financial services sector organization. They will intervene and try to find solutions to complaints.

▶ *The FSA also offers guidance on a range of financial services issues via their website: www.fsa.gov.uk.*

Typical complaints against banks tend to be about mis-selling of particular products, bank charges, mistakes made with direct debits and other automated payments, and security of data, among many other issues.

If you do need to complain about a financial services institution the standard process is:

▶ *Contact the institution first by phone or in writing explaining what your complaint is and what you want them to do about it. All the big institutions have details on their website of how to complain and what the process is. Most will promise an acknowledgement of your complaint within 24 hours and will then take a week or so to look into it before you get a written response with a proposed solution or an explanation.*
▶ *If you are still not happy you must contact them again and then the complaint is usually referred to a more senior person within the institution. Again there will be a set period of time in which they are required to respond in accordance with the Banking Code. You will then receive a response.*
▶ *If you are still not happy you then need to refer the case to the Financial Ombudsman Service. They too have stated timelines and will liaise with you and the institution to find a resolution.*
▶ *If you are still not happy then you will have to take your complaint to court if you think it is a case of being mis-sold a product or overcharged. At the same time, or as an alternative, you can switch institutions so at least they are not getting your custom any more.*

All of this can take weeks and you will need to be quite persistent. You should keep copies of all correspondence and all other evidence in support of your claim as you may need it even several months or years later.

TEN IMPORTANT THINGS TO REMEMBER

1 *Current accounts provide us with a safe place to keep our money, with instant access using a range of payment methods. This is a good deal despite the criticism that banks sometimes get.*

2 *There is a range of bank accounts and ways of operating them including current accounts, premium accounts, savings accounts, online and telephone banking.*

3 *Premium accounts are often not worth paying extra for.*

4 *Your bank account details are valuable so keep them safe and always report any unusual activity on your accounts.*

5 *You should keep a regular eye on your bank statements for budgeting and security purposes.*

6 *Banks will charge you for extra services or for not sticking to their rules. These charges can be quite high.*

7 *You should inform the bank immediately if you need to go over your authorized overdraft limit.*

8 *Direct debits and standing orders are a good way of budgeting.*

9 *There are legal and self-regulatory controls on the banks and how they deal with their customers.*

10 *You can try to claim back bank charges if you think they are too high or unfair.*

8

Tax, National Insurance and benefits

In this chapter you will learn:
- *the basic principles of personal taxation*
- *what income tax and National Insurance (NI) are*
- *what level of tax you should be paying based on your income*
- *what allowances are available to reduce the amount you are taxed*
- *what arrangements are available for the self-employed including self-assessment*
- *what Capital Gains Tax (CGT) and Inheritance Tax (IHT) are and who has to pay them*
- *how council tax works*
- *how VAT is calculated and what products and services are exempt*
- *what range of state benefits is available and whether you might be entitled to them*
- *ways in which you might be able to reduce the amount of tax you pay*

Introduction

'In this world nothing can be said to be certain, except death and taxes.'

Benjamin Franklin

According to the website unbiased.co.uk, only 16% of the UK population thinks that the UK tax system is fair. However, 81% of us don't do anything at all to improve our tax situation.

This chapter will look at the 'tax burden' on each individual. This is the total amount of income tax, National Insurance and all the so-called 'hidden taxes' where we are paying tax and duties on other things. It is difficult to estimate how much we spend on taxes as part of our income. We do know that the average UK resident pays 20% on their earnings and a further 11% in National Insurance. Add to that an estimated 17% of disposable income going on other taxes including council tax, VAT and petrol duties and you are losing about half your income.

Obviously we all benefit from paying into the tax system as it pays for key services such health, education, the police and the armed forces. We also have a system of **state benefits**, including the state pension, much of which is means-tested and some of which is available to people with particular circumstances, e.g. the elderly or families.

This chapter will explain the basics of how the tax and National Insurance system works and of ways in which you can reduce your personal tax burden. It will also look at the range of benefits that you might be entitled to.

Income tax and National Insurance (NI)

The biggest chunk that most of us pay is income tax and National Insurance (NI). Income tax pays for public services and NI entitles you to certain state benefits including your pension. The rules on income tax and NI are complex and vary depending on your personal circumstances. For example:

> ▶ *If you are over state pension age, which is currently 60 for women and 65 for men, you will pay a lower percentage of income tax and you do not have to pay NI at all.*

- ▶ *If you are self-employed and acting as a sole trader you will pay income tax and NI on account.*
- ▶ *If you own your own company you will have to work out your own tax and pay two sets of National Insurance contributions (NICs), one for yourself as an employee and one as the employer.*

This section will cover these eventualities and tell you where to get help and advice with your tax.

Most employees are paid monthly via a transaction made directly into the bank. This payment is what is called your 'net income' which is the amount you get once tax (and NI) has been taken off. This is done by your employer so you never actually get to see this money. By law, your employer must provide you with a pay slip, which explains how much you have been paid and also details your **tax code** and the amount that has been deducted for tax and NI. This system is often referred to as **PAYE** or **Pay As You Earn**. This is what is known as a progressive tax because rather than charging everyone a flat rate of tax, this system means that the more you earn the more tax you will pay. Many people think this is fairer because the tax you pay is based on your ability to pay it.

The amount of income tax or PAYE you pay is determined by your income and your tax code. There are three basic levels of income tax. Depending on your income you will either pay nothing, 20% or 40%.

Income	Tax rate
Starting rate for savings: £0 to £2,440	0%
Basic rate: £0 to £37,400	20%
Higher rate: over £37,400	40%

Before you can calculate how much tax you have to pay you need to look at your tax code, which determines how much you can earn before you have to start paying tax at all. Everyone has what are called '**allowances**'. These reduce the amount of tax that we have to pay.

The main one is the **personal allowance**, which in 2009/10 is £6,475. This means that you can earn up to £6,475 before you start paying any tax at all. You then pay 20% on everything you earn over this amount until you get to £37,400 at which point you pay the higher rate of 40%.

Looking at the three examples below:

Example 1

Mr A has a part-time job and earns £5,200 a year.
He pays no tax as he is below his personal allowance of £6,475.

Example 2

Mrs B has a full-time job and earns £32,000 a year.
She pays no tax on the first £6,475.
She then pays 20% on the remaining £25,525.
This means her total income tax for the year is £25,525 × 20% = £5,105.

Example 3

Mrs C has a full-time job and earns £50,000 a year.
She pays no tax on the first £6,475.
She then pays 20% on everything up to £37,400 which is where the higher rate kicks in. So she pays 20% on the difference between the higher tax limit and her personal allowance which is £37,400 − £6,475 = £30,925.
£30,925 × 20% = £6,185
She then has to pay 40% on everything she earns over £37,400, which is another £12,600.
£12,600 × 40% = £5,040
Her total tax burden is the two amounts added together.
£6,185 + £5,040 = £11,225

You will receive a notification of tax coding from your tax office every year on which you will be given a tax code. For most of us the tax code will be 647L. This is the standard tax code for people who are only entitled to the personal allowance of £6,475 a year and you can see that the first three digits indicate the amount. If you have a tax code of 703L you have additional allowances that mean you can earn up to £7,030 before you start paying tax.

There are many factors which can affect your allowance and it is worth checking on the government website that all allowances are being taken into account, or contact your tax office and inform them of your circumstances. For example, there are increased personal allowances, which therefore reduce the tax bill for:

▶ *people aged over 65*
▶ *married couples aged over 75*
▶ *blind people*
▶ *divorced or separated people paying maintenance.*

Insight

Mr D was surprised to find that he was still liable for income tax even though he had just retired and was aged 66. His income from his state pension and personal pension came to £15,000 a year. However, he was able to reduce his tax bill as his personal allowance was now £9,490 instead of £6,475 for the under-65s. His total tax bill was reduced by just over £600.

Some allowances are related to particular types of jobs. For example there are allowances, which therefore reduce the tax bill, for:

▶ *business mileage expenses*
▶ *some types of clothing and tools*
▶ *travel and subsistence costs*
▶ *household expenses if working from home.*

If you are an employee all of the PAYE and NI calculations will be done by someone in your office. If you work for a big company they may have a dedicated wages or payroll department. It is worth checking their calculations, particularly if you have just started a new job, or if you have had a change in salary or circumstances. Common mistakes that payroll departments make are:

▶ *Taxing you at Basic Rate (BR) because they do not know your tax code. This means that you will be paying too much tax as they have not taken your personal allowance into account. Make sure your employer sees your 'Notice of Tax Coding' document or P45 from your previous employer.*

▶ *Taxing you incorrectly by not taking into account earnings from a previous job. This can happen if you change jobs during the tax year. Your previous employer should have sent you a P45 when you left. If not, ask them for it.*

▶ *Using the wrong tax code. The tax code changes every year and you and your employer will get a letter from the tax office. You could be paying too much tax if your tax code is too low.*

▶ *Not taking allowances into account. You may be entitled to allowances, e.g. on company mileage, that the payroll department has forgotten to inform you or the tax office about. Check what allowances you are entitled to on the government website: http://www.direct.gov.uk/en/MoneyTax AndBenefits/Taxes/BeginnersGuideToTax/IncomeTax/ Taxallowancesandreliefs/index.htm.*

National Insurance works in a slightly different way. The exact amount will vary from year to year, but for the 2009/10 tax year everyone aged 16 and over and up to retirement age, who earns between £110 and £844 a week, pays National Insurance Contributions (NICs) at 11%. If you earn over £844 a week you pay an extra 1% on everything you earn. These are called 'Class 2' NICs.

Your NICs entitle you to certain benefits including your state pension. What this means is that if you have not made enough contributions over the years then you may not be entitled to full benefits. This is of particular importance in relation to the state pension. If you have not been working, perhaps due to bringing up children, then you may not have enough qualifying years to get your full pension. In the 2009/10 tax year the number of qualifying years was 44 for men and 39 for women. After April 2010 this is reduced to 30 years for men and women.

The difficulty is that you may not know whether or not you have a shortfall in your contributions so the best thing to do is contact the Pensions Service (http://www.thepensionservice.gov.uk/state-pension/forecast/home.asp) and ask for a state pension forecast. There is also a National Insurance Enquiry Helpline on 0845 915 5996. If you do think you are going to fall short you can pay voluntary contributions, which allow you to put enough into the pot to be entitled to your pension.

Tax and NI for the self-employed

The rules are quite different for the self-employed and it depends on whether you are a sole trader or operating as a limited company. The basic rules are explained here but for most businesses the best advice would be to get an accountant. This is because the rules change so often and you could find yourself with unexpected tax bills or even fines.

Accountants' charges vary enormously, but there are many who deal specifically with small businesses, and have cost structures accordingly. Charges start at about £700 a year but can get much higher than this. The general rule when taking on an accountant is that they should save you more money than you pay them.

As a sole trader you will pay income tax on your profits rather than on your income. This means that you do not have to operate a PAYE system. Therefore you are not paying tax on a regular basis,

but at the end of the year after you have worked out your profit. After your first year of trading you will be asked to pay lump sums on account calculated on previous years' profits.
In terms of NICs you will pay 'Class 2' NICs at a flat rate weekly amount of £2.40 and then 'Class 4' NICs as a percentage of your taxable profits. This is currently 8% on annual taxable profits between £5,715 and £43,875 and 1% on any taxable profit over that amount.

If you are a limited company then you will have to operate a PAYE scheme, even if you are the only employee. You will be sent a CD by HM Revenue and Customs with PAYE and NI calculators on it to help you. Effectively you will pay yourself a salary and then pay tax and NI on this as income. You will also pay Corporation Tax on any profits you make at the end of the year. Employers also have to pay 'Class 1' NI contributions for each of their employees which varies depending on income. Typically this would be 11%. You also have to pay an additional Employers' NI contribution.

Self-assessment

If you are self-employed you will be asked to complete a **self-assessment** tax return. Other people may also be asked to do this if they have complicated tax affairs or if tax cannot be collected through the normal PAYE system, for example if you earn money abroad.

A **tax return** is a paper or on-line form that asks you about all your forms of income and allows you to claim your full allowances. They are normally sent to you in April and have to be completed by the end of October for paper-based forms or the end of the following January if you do it online.

Completing the tax return can be quite complicated and you will need to find all the relevant figures for all forms of income and some of your expenditure. You will need to allow plenty of time to complete it. Further information is available on the government website: http://www.hmrc.gov.uk/sa/introduction.htm.

Capital Gains Tax (CGT)

Capital Gains Tax is paid on an asset that you sell or give away that has increased in value since you bought it. It only applies to certain assets and it only kicks in if the amount you have made exceeds a certain amount.

Perhaps the most common form of CGT is if you own more than one property and then you sell one of your properties. If you have made money on the sale of the second property then you will have to pay CGT on the profit, which is currently 18%.

The basic rules based on the 2009/10 tax year are:

▶ *You do not have to pay CGT on any gain less than £10,100 (per individual).*
▶ *You do not have to pay CGT on any asset worth less than £6,000.*

- *You do not pay CGT on the sale of your house if you only own one house.*
- *You do not have to pay CGT on the sale of cars.*

If you are liable for CGT you will normally be asked to complete a self-assessment tax return.

Many people come into contact with CGT after the death of a relative where a house is passed on in the will. At the time of death, CGT is not payable but when the asset is subsequently sold, the CGT then becomes payable based on the difference between the market value at the time of death and the amount that it sells for. It is the recipient of the money from the sale that is liable for the CGT. Therefore, if you sell your deceased parent's home, for example, you will have to pay 18% of the proceeds in CGT.

You are allowed to transfer assets to your partner or spouse as you each effectively have an allowance of £10,100 before you have to start paying, However, you are not allowed to avoid CGT by passing assets to your children.

Council tax

Council tax has been one of the most contentious of taxes over recent years. This is because whereas some taxes stay around the same or even go down in percentage terms over the years, council tax has more than doubled in the last decade.

Council tax is payable by every household rather than the individuals within them, with the amount payable based notionally on the value of the house. Revenues from council tax go to pay for local services including education, refuse collection, roads and policing.

The council tax is an annual tax bill, which local councils will send to you. Each council is allowed to set the rate of council tax within certain government constraints. You can arrange to pay this in one lump sum or split into monthly payments over the year. The amount payable varies from council to council but is based on a valuation of your home. These are based on valuations the government did in the early 1990s when the system was first introduced.

For 2009/10 the bands are:

Band A ... up to £40,000
Band B ... £40,001 to £52,000
Band C ... £52,001 to £68,000
Band D ... £68,001 to £88,000
Band E ... £88,001 to £120,000
Band F ... £120,001 to £160,000
Band G ... £160,001 to £320,000
Band H ... £320,001 and above

The valuations are done by a government agency (Valuation Office Agency) and more details of how they are calculated, including the amounts payable in each council area in each band can be found at: http://www.voa.gov.uk/council_tax/index.htm.

Inheritance Tax (IHT)

Inheritance Tax is the amount paid to the government on your death based on the value of everything you own when you die. So we have death and taxes at the same time in this scenario. The amount payable is 40% tax on everything over the current limit of £325,000.

It is typically the executor of the will that will have to make arrangements to pay any Inheritance Tax due. Within six months of the death, it is the executor's job to have the estate valued. This includes everything the person owned including property, other assets and amounts paid from insurance policies. If this comes to more than £325,000 then there are forms to fill in so that the 40% can be paid on the excess.

Inheritance Tax can get complex and full details can be found at:
http://www.direct.gov.uk/en/MoneyTaxAndBenefits/
Taxes/InheritanceTaxEstatesAndTrusts/DG_4016736.

There are a number of exemptions to IHT, the main one being that if the deceased is survived by their partner or spouse, then IHT is not payable. There are also exemptions if the deceased gifted part of their estate several years before they died. The common way to do this is to gift assets to people within a trust. There are special rules that apply to parts of the estate held in trust.

There is a whole branch of financial planning that has emerged around IHT, as an increasing number of people are now likely to leave estates worth more than £325,000 due to the increase in house prices over recent years. The idea of IHT planning is to distribute your wealth to the people you want to have it while you are alive. This reduces the value of your estate so there will be less IHT to pay. This enables you to pass on more of your wealth to your family.

One key part of planning that you should do is to make a will. A solicitor will do a simple will for less than £100 and it does mean that you have left very clear instructions as to how you want your estate divided up when you die. It gives you peace of mind while you are alive to know that you are not leaving a mess for your relatives or friends to sort out.

Value Added Tax (VAT)

Value Added Tax is a tax payable on most goods and services. It is usually, but not always included in the price of whatever it is we are buying. At the time of writing the rate of VAT is 17.5%, which means that 17.5% of the price we pay goes to the government in tax. The VAT rate was reduced to 15% in 2008 to try to stimulate the economy during recession. The VAT rate went back up to 17.5% on 1 January 2010.

Some things we buy are quoted ex-VAT, which means you have to add 17.5% to the price to find out what the real price is. This has become a common trick, particularly on the Internet where you might be buying products that look cheaper than others because they are quoted without the VAT.

Some products and services have a reduced rate of VAT or are exempt altogether because the government considers them important and therefore unfair or unwise to add VAT.

Reduced VAT goods and services have a 5% VAT rate and examples include:

▶ *domestic energy supplies*
▶ *installation of energy saving products*
▶ *women's sanitary products*
▶ *child car seats.*

Examples of zero-rated VAT goods and services include:

▶ *food*
▶ *sewerage services and water supply*
▶ *books*
▶ *drugs and medicines.*

A full list of exemptions can be obtained from: http://www.direct.gov.uk/en/MoneyTaxAndBenefits/Taxes.

Benefits

There is a whole range of state benefits that you may be entitled to. The state benefit system is designed to help the most vulnerable people in our society including people:

▶ *on a low income*
▶ *with dependent children*

- *who are ill or disabled*
- *who are caring for someone*
- *aged 60 or over*
- *who have been bereaved*
- *who are pregnant or have recently had a baby.*

Benefits are designed to be paid out when they are needed and most are means-tested to ensure that the person is in need. Some state benefits cover quite specific circumstances and a full list is available at: http://ukonline.direct.gov.uk/en/MoneyTaxAndBenefits/ BenefitsTaxCreditsAndOtherSupport/ BeginnersGuideToBenefits/index.htm.

In this section we will take a look at some of the most common benefits, summarizing who is eligible, how much you get and where to find out more. Remember that the amounts will change every financial year and occasionally benefits do get withdrawn completely or replaced with new ones.

Various different government departments are involved with benefits. Most benefits related to employment are administered through the Department for Work and Pensions (DWP): http:// www.dwp.gov.uk/. They are distributed through their Jobcentre Plus offices: http://www.jobcentreplus.gov.uk/JCP/index.html. In other cases payments are made via HM Revenue and Customs, through Post Offices or by direct payments into your bank account.

Name of benefit	Eligibility	How much	More information
Jobseeker's allowance	Aged 16–60 and work less than 16 hours a week and actively seeking work.	Up to £64.30 a week per person	Jobcentre Plus: http://www.jobcentreplus.gov.uk
Income support	Aged 16–60 and work less than 16 hours week. Have a low income but cannot actively seek work due to personal circumstances.	Up to £64.30 a week per person.	Jobcentre Plus: http://www.jobcentreplus.gov.uk
Tax credits	Aged 16+ and are employed or self-employed and care for one or more children.	Varies depending on personal circumstances including other income and benefits.	http://www.taxcredits.inlandrevenue. gov.uk/Quality/WhatAreTaxCredits.aspx
Child benefit	Payable to the parent or parents of children aged up 16 or in some cases 18.	£20 per week for the first child; £13.20 a week for other children.	http://www.hmrc.gov.uk/childbenefit

(Contd)

Name of benefit	Eligibility	How much	More information
Incapacity benefit	Payable if you are unable to work due to illness or disability starting before 27/10/2008.	Up to £89.80 a week depending on circumstances and length of time that you are unable to work.	http://www.dwp.gov.uk
Employment and support allowance	Replaced incapacity benefit for new claimants after 27/10/2008.	Up to £95.15 a week depending on circumstances and length of time that you are unable to work.	http://www.direct.gov.uk/en/DisabledPeople/FinancialSupport/esa/index.htm
Housing benefit	Your rent is payable if you are on a low income and have savings of less than £16,000.	Up to the total of your rent.	http://www.direct.gov.uk

Name of benefit	Eligibility	How much	More information
Council tax benefit	Payable if you are on a low income and have less than £16,000 savings.	Up to 100% of your council tax bill paid depending on personal circumstances.	http://www.direct.gov.uk
Pension credit	Payable if you are over 60 and on a low income, currently £198.45 a week for couples or £130 for people living on their own.	Your weekly income is made up to £198.45 for couples and £130 for people living on their own.	http://www.thepensionservice.gov.uk
State pensions	Payable to women over 60 and men over 65.	Up to £95.25 per week for a single pensioner depending on circumstances and NI contributions	http://www.thepensionservice.gov.uk

As a note of caution, sometimes people accidently carry on claiming benefits after their circumstances change. If this happens you will probably have to pay back all the benefits you have claimed and possibly pay a fine. If it is considered that you have been doing this on purpose you are liable for prosecution. As a rule, every time your circumstances change you should inform the appropriate government department.

Unfortunately the state system does attract benefits cheats who see it as a way of claiming money for nothing. If you suspect someone is deliberately cheating the system you can report them to the Department for Work and Pensions at: http://campaigns.dwp.gov.uk/campaigns/benefit-thieves/.

Tax savings

Your individual tax and benefits affairs can get very complex and the rules are complicated and change all the time. There are a few simple things that we can all do to ensure that we are not paying too much tax and that you are getting all the benefits you are entitled to:

▶ *Check your notice of tax coding to ensure that you are getting all the allowances you are entitled to.*
▶ *Check that your employer is using the correct tax code on your pay slip.*
▶ *If you have savings, make sure you are using your annual tax free allowance through an ISA.*
▶ *If you have children, make sure you are claiming child benefit, that you invest your children's bond and that you make the most of their allowance for savings, perhaps through a child savings bond.*
▶ *Check whether you are entitled to any benefits particularly if you are on a low income, are over 60, are ill or disabled or are caring for someone else.*

- *If you have paid too much tax, claim it back by contacting your tax office (shown on your notice of tax coding).*
- *Make sure you are not paying NICs after the age of 60. If you have, claim them back.*
- *Think about investing spare income into a private pension scheme. Effectively every pound you put in is worth £1.28 as you do not pay tax on it.*
- *If you are married and your partner earns less than you, put your savings in the name of the lower earner.*

Finally, it is worth mentioning that there is a massive difference between 'tax evasion' and 'tax avoidance'. Tax evasion is the deliberate act of not paying tax, which is illegal and can lead to fines and imprisonment. Tax avoidance is about operating within the law to ensure that you avoid paying as much tax as possible.

TEN IMPORTANT THINGS TO REMEMBER

1 We all pay taxes, either directly through our income, or indirectly through other taxes such as VAT.

2 If you are employed you will pay income tax in the form of PAYE and National Insurance contributions on your income.

3 If you are on a low income you may not have to pay any income tax. If you are on a high income you will pay a higher percentage of income tax.

4 We are all entitled to allowances which reduce our income tax liability.

5 Your notice of tax coding indicates how much money you can earn before you start paying tax. You should check that your employer is using the correct coding.

6 If you are self-employed there is a different system for collecting tax and NI.

7 Capital Gains Tax and Inheritance Tax are payable if you sell certain assets at a profit, or inherit over a certain amount.

8 VAT is payable on most goods and services and adds 17.5% to the price.

9 Council tax is payable by the household as a whole rather than the individual and is based on the value of the house.

10 There is a range of state benefits that you may be entitled to, particularly if you are a parent, elderly, ill or disabled or a carer.

9

Buying financial products and services

In this chapter you will learn:
- *how to buy financial services and products*
- *how to shop around to find the best deal*
- *how to use price comparison websites and what to watch out for when you do*
- *how to switch providers*
- *what rights you have as a consumer*
- *how credit referencing works and how you can find out your personal credit history*
- *what financial advice is available and how to choose a financial adviser*
- *what scams are out there and how to avoid becoming a victim*

Introduction

Most of us spend quite a lot of time shopping around for the best deal. The more expensive the product, the more time we tend to spend looking into the alternatives. We may go to several websites and shops to check what we can get for our money. In fact, the retail world knows we do this, which is why you find, for example, all the car showrooms or large DIY stores in the same part of town. They know that we want to carry out some 'comparison shopping' and so conveniently locate themselves next to their biggest rivals.

Most of us have got quite good at comparison shopping and do it with cars, electrical items, computers, clothes, petrol and even food. However, we are not so good at doing it with financial products. This is probably because buying financial products is not as much fun. However, we stand to save large amounts of money if we can be bothered to do it.

Just to be clear on the terminology, the banks tend to refer to 'products' when they are talking about their off-the-shelf offerings such as mortgages, loans, bank accounts, insurance etc. A 'service' is something that they will do for you, usually at extra cost, such as exchange foreign currency or cancel a cheque. Other financial services include things like financial advice. For the purposes of this chapter we are referring to any product or service that you might purchase from any type of provider.

In many ways, buying financial products is just like buying any other kind of product:

▶ *You shop around for the best deal.*
▶ *You get persuaded by adverts and promotions.*
▶ *You have legal rights to ensure the product is fit for purpose.*
▶ *You make your choice and pay your money.*

With financial products there are some extra factors to take into consideration:

▶ *You can seek out the help and advice of a specialist financial adviser.*
▶ *You can switch products at almost any time and as often as you like.*
▶ *You have extra legal protection in the way that financial products and services are sold.*
▶ *You may want to buy a financial product but be refused because of your* **credit rating**.
▶ *You might be the victim of a fraud or* **scam**.

This chapter will look at all of these factors and give general advice on how to buy financial products and services.

Shopping around

The first stage of the process is to shop around and many of us simply don't do this. The banks know that many of us are quite loyal (or it could be lazy!) and that we are likely to stick with the same bank that we have had for years. Many people still bank with whomever they had a children's account with. This is not necessarily a bad thing but it might be worth checking out what else is on offer. The world of financial services is highly competitive and never more so than in the middle or at the end of a recession.

Another phenomenon at work here is that a lot of us will use the same institutions for all of our products. For example, if we get a mortgage from a bank, we will probably use them for the house insurance. After that we then buy their home and contents insurance and open a savings account. Again, this is not necessarily a bad thing, but generally speaking you will not be rewarded for your loyalty. In fact, many offers are only available to new customers.

There are three main problems with shopping around:

The first is that it is time-consuming and, with busy lives, many of us simply can't be bothered to shop around before buying a financial product. Sometimes this will depend on the value of the product that you are buying. If you are buying travel insurance and the first two quotes are for £30 and £35 you may not think that it is worth spending ages looking for any more deals and you would probably be right. However, high-value financial products such as mortgages and pensions cost us a lot of money. You could end up paying thousands of pounds in interest payments on a mortgage over the years, or paying thousands of pounds into a pension.

In these cases, some time spent at the beginning might save or gain you thousands of pounds over the life of the product.

The second factor is that things are constantly changing. For example, you might move your money into a savings account one week because it is in the 'best buy' tables in your newspaper only to find within a few weeks that there are a dozen better deals on offer. If this is the case you can think about switching.

The third factor is the difficulty of comparing like with like. The Financial Services Authority (FSA) is the body in charge of regulating the banks and they do have strict rules designed to help us compare products. One example of this is the APR and AER that we came across in Chapters 3 and 4. They also have rules about how the financial institutions advertise potential returns on investments looking at typical returns given different rates of interest. More details at www.moneymadeclear.fsa.gov.uk.

Insight

When shopping around for a private pension, Mr B tried several large insurance companies. Two of the companies were prepared to send advisers to his house, although he found that the arrangement and management fees reflected this personal service. The other companies did not offer any advice, which meant he had to know what he was buying. In the end he did a lot of research himself choosing a provider that had relatively low management fees and reasonably good performance over the last ten years. However, he won't know for another 25 years whether he made the right decision!

Much of this comes down to how much time you want to spend shopping around and how much research you want to do into the different companies that you might deal with. There are some general guidelines you can follow, many of which are common to any type of purchase you might make:

▶ *Ask family and friends about who they use for various products and services and go on recommendation.*

► *Consider using the large, well-known companies who have a reputation to maintain and who are less likely to get into trouble if the economy is in trouble.*

► *Consider using the same company that you already use for another financial product.*

► *Consider using an Independent Financial Adviser, particularly if they come recommended. (More on this later.)*

► *Do your own research using the Internet, specialist magazines or the money sections of the newspapers.*

► *Look at the APR/AER/charge structure of the product you are buying as a way of comparing. For example, if you are investing money, you will be charged a* **management fee**, *usually shown as a percentage.*

► *Avoid deals from companies that you don't know that appear too good to be true. (More on scams later.)*

► *Read the small print, checking for restrictive conditions such as minimum contracts or penalty charges for cancellation.*

► *Decide what features are important to you and buy based on need. Don't be enticed by free pens!*

Price comparison websites

There is now a **price comparison website** for almost everything. Financial products and services ones are particularly useful as there are so many financial services organizations to choose from. You can let the comparison site do the work for you. Comparison sites can save you lots of time and money, just as they say in their adverts. However, it is worth knowing how they work and how they make their money so that you can make an informed decision. It's also worth remembering that some financial services companies, including some of the big ones, are not listed on comparison websites and that no one comparison site covers the whole market.

In simple terms, a comparison website lists the details of hundreds of different financial products from a range of providers. These are categorized under main headings, e.g. car insurance, mortgages, loans, etc. You register your personal details with the website and then do a search for what it is you are looking for. In some cases you may have to provide quite a lot of information. It then searches through all the deals and generates a list in descending price order. You can then read basic information on the site or click directly onto the website of the provider where you can get more detail and go on to buy the product.

If you take car insurance as an example you do have to type in four or five screens of information about you and your car before you get to the quotes. However, this is significantly quicker than going round, or phoning round all of the insurance companies and brokers to get different quotes.

It is estimated that the price comparison industry is worth up to £1 billion with the comparison websites making their money in commission from the financial services websites that they refer. This works in two main ways. The first is that the comparison website gets paid as if they were an agent or broker. For every client that a financial services company gets they will pay the comparison site. An alternative is a 'click-through' system where the comparison website gets paid if someone goes onto the financial services website through the comparison site.

This means that financial services companies do deals with the price comparison sites to get more customers. Often this can be to our benefit as it means that the financial services company will offer special deals with certain comparison websites to ensure that they come out high in the listing. It also means that you might get different quotes from the same financial services company through different comparison websites. The net result of this is that it pays to use more than one comparison website when shopping around. An unfortunate consequence of this is that you might find yourself getting unsolicited phone calls and emails from the financial services companies.

There is some discussion about other tricks that financial services companies might use to ensure that they get to the top of the listings.

One of these is particularly relevant to insurance where the providers strip out a lot of the features of their insurance to make it appear cheaper. For example, with car insurance, the provider might show a low price that has a high excess. Therefore if you did have to claim, you might find yourself having to pay the first £500 or more.

Insight

Mrs W was looking to put her 17-year-old son onto her car insurance. She found a deal on one of the well-known comparison sites with one insurer quoting 30% less than anything else she could find including the quote she got by going direct to that same insurance company. The only downside was a handful of unsolicited emails and phone calls.

The best advice here is to be as sceptical when using comparison sites as you would be when buying any other kind of product or service. These sites are basically salespeople for the providers and they make money on commission. It's the same relationship as a salesperson trying to sell you a car – you need to have your wits about you.

Switching

Switching is the process of swapping one product for another usually from a different provider. This has always been around but it has become a much bigger aspect of financial services in recent years. This is partly due to the widespread use of the Internet, which has made it easier to get information about other deals and has made the physical process much easier. On the utilities side, switching has come about due to the privatization and deregulation of the utility companies.

Whether you choose to switch or not comes down to many of the same issues that you faced when you were shopping around in the first place. There are undoubtedly savings to be made as there is so much competition. One of the difficulties is that the deals change so often that you would have to switch on a very regular basis to ensure that you always have the best deal.

With some products you can switch at any time. However, increasingly, the providers are making it more difficult to switch by tying you in to the better deals. For example:

▶ *Many utility companies and mobile phone contracts have minimum periods. These can be as much as two years.*
▶ *Attractive deals on savings accounts and bonds will usually require you to leave your money in for a set period of time or lose part or all of the interest payments.*
▶ *Some credit cards charge a fee for switching.*

Common products which you might be able to switch at any time are the mortgage, credit cards, loans and savings accounts. The process of switching is similar to buying the product in the first place, although it is worth checking on penalty clauses for cancelling the old product or arrangement fees for the new product.

Insurance products such as motor and house insurance tend to be switched when they are due for renewal, which is normally once a year. At that time, it pays to shop around again as your current provider will not necessarily be the best deal. If you are paying on monthly deals you may choose to switch during the year, but there is usually an additional administrative charge for this which you need to factor in when working out the costs. Also bear in mind that if you cancel a motor insurance policy before it runs out, you will not get that year added to your no-claims discount.

You can switch your gas, electricity, phones, TV and Internet providers. Gas and electricity prices in particular can vary enormously throughout the year as we saw in Chapter 6. Many providers are now offering fixed deals which tie you in to them for several months or years, but you do have a guarantee that the price will not go beyond a certain limit. This is particularly advantageous if you are on a tight budget and would prefer to know where you stand.

Just as when you shop around in the first place, the comparison websites are a useful tool here to help you find the best deal. Many will allow you to put in the details of your current spending and list the results from providers who can beat your current deal.

You should remember that there is a degree of hassle when switching as you will have to complete the necessary forms and cancel old direct debits and set up new ones. Unless you are particularly frugal, you may not choose to spend lots of your personal time sniffing out a deal that is only slightly better than the one you are on. However, it is worth considering switching at key times, for example:

▶ *When your current deal or rate runs out, e.g. mortgage and savings rates, or 0% interest rates on credit cards.*
▶ *When it is time to renew, e.g. an insurance policy.*
▶ *At fixed times during the year, e.g. consider doing an annual review of all your finances in one go.*
▶ *If you are not happy with the service you are getting.*
▶ *When there are changes in the market, e.g. if oil prices go down leading to a large reduction in gas and electricity prices or if the government announces changes in tax rates.*

Consumer rights

We have certain rights as a consumer (**consumer rights**) which apply to all the products and services we buy. In addition, there is some specific legislation relating to financial products and services. These are overseen by various government departments and **watchdog** organizations:

▶ **The Financial Services Authority (FSA)** – *www.fsa.gov.uk or www.moneymadeclear.fsa.gov – regulator of the financial services companies. These authorize businesses and individuals to ensure that they are trustworthy, give good advice and have a complaints procedure for if things go wrong.*

- **Office of Fair Trading (OFT)** – _www.oft.gov.uk_ – *consumer rights for any kind of shopping. In particular, they regulate businesses that lend money to ensure that they are trustworthy and that they give you the information you need to make a decision when borrowing money.*
- **Trading Standards** – _www.tradingstandards.gov.uk_ – *advice and protection when buying products and services and pursue 'rogue' traders.*
- **Department for Business Innovation and Skills** – _www.berr.gov.uk_ – *formerly the DTI, they oversee the Sale of Goods Act, which ensures that products and services sold to you are fit for purpose.*
- **Industry regulators** – *specific 'watchdog' organizations exist for each of the utility industries if you have issues relating to supply or prices:*
  - **Water industry (Ofwat)** – _www.ofwat.gov.uk_
  - **Gas and electricity industry (Ofgem)** – _www.ofgem.gov.uk_
  - **Communications industry (TV, Internet and phone)** – _www.ofcom.org.uk_.

A good website which gives an overview of all of your rights including links to the organizations listed above is: http://www.consumerdirect.gov.uk/. These organizations are your first port of call for advice, information and details of how to complain when something goes wrong.

Most financial services companies, including all the larger well-known ones are authorized by the FSA. This means that they must operate within specific guidelines set down by the authority. As a general rule of thumb, you should not deal with any financial services organization or adviser who is not registered with the FSA. The FSA publish a register at: http://www.moneymadeclear.fsa.gov.uk/tools/check_our_register.html.

Specific legislation in the form of the **Consumer Credit Act** covers any circumstance where you are being lent money. Almost all organizations that lend money have to be licensed by the OFT. Full details of the act are available from the OFT but in essence the law ensures that you are given sufficient information, that the APR is clearly stated, that you have a chance to change your mind (the 'cooling off' period) and that charges are fair.

The advantage of dealing with organizations who are registered with the FSA or licensed by the OFT is that they provide you with legal protection, not least access to the Financial Services Compensation Scheme, if the organization goes bankrupt while still holding on to your money. This covers you for £50,000 of savings per institution. The other main advantage is these businesses and individuals have to have a complaints procedure, which involves the Financial Ombudsman Service for when disputes can't be settled. Details of **complaints procedures** have to be clearly stated and have a set timeline.

Without going into the detail of the procedure here, if you do need to complain a few useful tips are:

▶ *Do it in writing (paper or email) so that you have a record.*
▶ *Find a named individual to deal with.*
▶ *Keep all correspondence and all evidence of your complaint, e.g. statements showing over-charging.*
▶ *Be patient and persistent – it could take weeks.*

Credit referencing

Credit referencing is the process of checking your financial history when an organization is deciding whether or not to lend you money. The logic behind this is that credit is a privilege and not a right and that organizations that lend money are well within their rights to check you out. In fact, it is the responsible thing to do to ensure that you are not borrowing beyond your means. The problems occur when we get refused credit and this is why the credit referencing agencies sometimes get a bad press.

In our lifetimes we will probably be credit checked hundreds of times. Every time you apply for anything that involves getting credit, for example a mortgage, loan, overdraft or credit card you will be credit checked. Even if you go onto a mobile phone contract you will be checked as the mobile phone company will want to check that you can afford the monthly payments. Also, the more you switch the more you will get checked.

Credit referencing agencies look at a number of factors when assessing your 'credit worthiness', including time at address, previous credit history, whether you are a home owner, age and employment status. The agencies get this information from various sources although the main source of information comes from all of the banks, building societies and other providers who pool information on customers.

They use a system called 'credit scoring' where you get points for factors that they think mean you are a good risk. For example, if you are not on the electoral roll you will get a low score. If you have any county court judgments (CCJs) for non-payment of previous debts, you will get a low score. If you have borrowed money before and paid it back you will get a high score. If you own your own home you will get a higher score.

Credit decisions are usually made fairly quickly, in some cases within a minute or two. In some cases you may be refused credit and in other cases you may be charged a higher APR on borrowing to reflect a higher level of risk. It is the money-lending organization that makes the final decision and they all operate their own scoring systems. If you do get refused credit, or get offered a higher APR than the typical rate on offer, it is not always easy to find out why.

You can check what information the credit referencing agencies hold about you by paying a small fee. You can do this in writing or online. The three main agencies are:

- *Experian: www.experian.com*
- *Equifax: www.equifax.xo.uk*
- *Callcredit: www.callcredit.co.uk*

If you find that the information they hold about you is incorrect then you have the right to ask them to correct it which they must do within a set time frame.

What all this means is that your credit history is important in terms of your future borrowing. The best customers as far as the lenders are concerned are those that borrow a lot but always pay it back. These are the customers who will get the best rates. If you don't have much of a credit history because you have never borrowed money or if you have a bad credit history, you may get refused or charged a higher APR. There is no simple solution to this in the short term, but your credit score will change over time every time you borrow money.

Financial advisers

A financial adviser is someone who gets paid to give you advice on any aspect of finance. These can be particularly useful for more complex financial products such as mortgages, pensions and investments. It is worth noting that the FSA are planning changes to the way in which financial advisers are paid commission. These changes are planned for 2012. In the meantime, there are two main types of adviser:

Independent financial advisers (IFAs) operate entirely independently from the financial services organizations that they might recommend. These normally charge a fee for their advice, or will take a commission from the organization they recommend if you go on to buy the product. They may do both.

Tied advisers work for specific organizations and are only able to recommend products offered by that organization. These advisers are normally full-time members of staff who are salaried and will be paid bonuses on top based on sales. A variation on this is a **multi-tied adviser** who is able to offer products from a range of providers.

This leaves us with an age-old problem in terms of giving financial advice:

▶ *Can the independent adviser be truly independent if they are reliant on the providers for commission? Surely they will recommend the one that pays them the biggest commission?*
▶ *Can the tied adviser offer you the best deal when they only have a limited number of products on offer?*

There is no easy answer to these questions, but there is some protection in place provided by the FSA who regulate independent financial advisers (IFAs). Make sure your IFA is FSA registered as it has the following benefits:

▶ *The IFA must tell you whether they are independent, tied or multi-tied so that you know whether they are looking at all products or just those of the organization they are tied to.*
▶ *They must clearly state what their charges are going to be if they charge a fee, or state what their commission is from the provider. This means that you can see whether they are simply recommending the one with the biggest commission.*
▶ *They must tell you what qualification they have. This enables you to decide whether they are qualified to give advice in specific areas. For example, some IFAs specialize in investments but may not be up-to-date on the mortgage market.*
▶ *They must ask you about your attitude to risk. This is to ensure that they are not steering you towards products that carry a higher (or lower) risk than you want to take.*

Choosing an IFA can be difficult. It is best to go on recommendation if you can. There is a register of IFAs at www.unbiased.co.uk along with advice on how to choose one and what to do if there are any problems.

Insight

Mrs W wanted an IFA to help her set up a private pension plan. She had tried going to the big insurance companies direct but they were only able to talk about their own products. She tried three. The first was not registered with the FSA and without asking any questions, advised her towards a particular provider. The second came to see her in her home and offered to put some quotes together based on a detailed discussion for a fee of £200. The third also discussed her needs and offered to put some quotes together from several companies for free and would then take his commission from the one that she chose, or put further quotes together until she was satisfied. She chose the third IFA.

Scams and identity theft

Finally in this chapter is a note of caution. Up to now we have been looking at legitimate businesses operating within the law. However, we do need to be aware that there are some out-and-out criminals out there who are just trying to steal our money and/or our identities.

Scams come and go and criminals are always thinking of ways to try to extract our money from us. Some scams are designed to get our money, while others are aimed at obtaining personal information, which in turn will be used fraudulently to make money. The financial services industry as a whole reacts when they are aware that a new scam is out there. In this section we will look at some of the common ones doing the rounds and how you can minimize the risk of becoming a victim.

Boiler room scams: These are unsolicited offers from 'boiler room' brokers to buy shares in businesses. The shares are offered at apparently low rates with plausible reasons as to why they are going to rocket within the next few months. These scamsters target people who they know already trade in the stock market and are able to talk in an authoritative way about the market. Sometimes they are prepared to play a long game by starting small and then building up your investment over a period of months making them even more convincing. In some cases, the 'boiler room' company that contacted you will simply disappear with your money. In other cases, you will find yourself with lots of shares in a worthless company.

To avoid this:

▶ *Don't be tempted by offers that come out of the blue and appear too good to be true.*
▶ *Check that the broker is registered with the FSA.*
▶ *Use the services of an IFA to check the investment.*
▶ *Do your own research on the broker and on the company whose shares they are tipping.*
▶ *Don't be pressured.*

Phishing: This is the process of getting you to part with your bank account details. It is done by sending you an email that looks like it is from your bank. There will be some plausible reason why they need your bank account details, which they ask you to email back to them. Some are quite sophisticated and link you to a website that will look like your bank's website and even have a similar web address. On this site you will be asked to input your details. The scamsters will then take your bank details and use it either to take money from your bank account or to carry out some fraudulent act. They may also sell your details on to other criminals.

To avoid this:

▶ *Your bank will never ask for your bank account details via email so if you get asked – it's a scam.*
▶ *Delete all emails that you are suspicious about before opening them if possible.*
▶ *Never open an attachment or click on a link within an email if you are unsure about it. Even doing this can give the criminals information about your computer.*
▶ *Consider having a separate bank account which you use for online purchases. Only have a small amount of money in it.*
▶ *Keep a regular eye on your bank account to check for unusual activity.*

Email offers: These are emails that you will receive using a range of creative reasons for why you need to send some money off. Typical examples are that you have won some money in a competition, or are entitled to an amazing gift. All you have to do is send a small amount to get your hands on it. Another approach plays on your charitable nature in that someone from a poor country is trying to get funds released for some noble cause and that they will pay you if you help them. Often these offers are very convincing. A fuller list of common scams is available via the OFT at: http://www.consumerdirect.gov.uk/watch_out/ Commonscams/ID theft.

To avoid this:

▶ *If an offer is too good to be true, it's usually because it is. Ignore it.*
▶ *Avoid offers that come out of the blue particularly if they are linked to some organization you have never heard of or are from some competition you have never entered.*
▶ *Do not respond to these offers or disclose any personal information of any sort.*

Identify theft is worth a special mention here. Statistics suggest that one in four of us has had their identity stolen or knows someone who has. The usual consequence of this is that we have either had money taken from out bank accounts, or that further borrowing has taken place in our name. One of the problems with identity theft is that there can be quite a time delay between our details getting stolen and us noticing that something has gone wrong.

Your ID can be stolen any time the information is used. This could be on printed documents in your house, the mail or even in the bin. It could also be on electronic communications or stored on websites.

To avoid this:

▶ *Keep documents in a safe place in your house. Don't bin documents with financial information on. Shred them or burn them.*

- ▶ *Keep your plastic cards safe and report it the second they are lost or stolen.*
- ▶ *Check your bank account regularly and inform the bank immediately if you suspect any irregularities.*
- ▶ *Check your credit history regularly to make sure there are no credit checks that you did not instigate.*
- ▶ *Inform the post office if you move house and have your mail redirected.*
- ▶ *Keep passwords and PINs safe and use different ones for different accounts.*
- ▶ *Change your passwords on a regular basis.*

A useful website set up by the government and other agencies is available at: http://www.identitytheft.org.uk.

TEN USEFUL THINGS TO REMEMBER

1 *Shopping around for financial products and services can save you hundreds of pounds.*

2 *Lots of advice is available when buying financial products and services.*

3 *You have to be quite sceptical and do your own research as it is not always easy to get 100% impartial advice.*

4 *You should research purchasing decisions carefully and consider using an IFA for more complex decisions such as pensions and investments.*

5 *Price comparison websites can save you time and money although you do need to be slightly wary about how they work.*

6 *Switching providers can save you lots of money and it does not necessarily pay to stay loyal to one provider.*

7 *It is worth considering switching if there are major changes in the market, or if your product is due for renewal.*

8 *You should only really consider dealing with companies and individuals registered with the FSA or licensed by the OFT.*

9 *You have quite a lot of legal protection in relation to financial services.*

10 *You should always be on the lookout for scams as there are lots of them and new ones come along all the time.*

10

Dealing with debt

In this chapter you will learn:
- *the difference between debt management and debt crisis*
- *how to manage debts*
- *how to get out of debt*
- *how to find out whether you are in debt crisis*
- *how to get out of debt crisis*
- *how to set up an Individual Voluntary Arrangement (IVA) or declare yourself bankrupt*
- *what sources of help and advice there are for dealing with debt*

Introduction

There is a tendency to think of all debts as a bad thing, but this is not necessarily the case. For example, very few of us could afford to buy our own houses without taking on an enormous debt in the form of a mortgage. There are other occasions in life when we choose to take on debts to get what we want now, and then manage the debt over the coming months and years.

Much of this comes down to your own personal attitude towards borrowing money. Some people steadfastly refuse to take on loans or credit cards, while others would never dream of saving up for something when they can get it now, even if it means paying extra for it in the long run.

There are two main aspects to debt:

▶ **Debt management:** *where you take on borrowing and build it into your budget paying it back in regular instalments.*
▶ **Debt crisis:** *where you can no longer afford to pay off your debts and are unable to make the basic monthly payments.*

This chapter will look at both aspects and in particular how to avoid getting into debt crisis, and how you may be able to get yourself out of it. With an increasing number of people getting into crisis, the financial sector has responded by offering financial products and services specifically for this market. In addition, there is help available from government and charitable organizations.

The national statistics on debt would indicate that the majority of us are in debt and that it is a significant factor in our everyday lives. The money charity Credit Action (www.creditaction.org.uk) collects a range of statistics each month on the levels and impact of debt in the UK. Some of their key findings at the time of writing were:

▶ *Over 2,000 county court judgments (CCJs) were issued in the last quarter of 2008.*
▶ *33,600 applications for credit have been turned down in the last six months.*
▶ *Over £1 billion of plastic card transactions take place every day.*

Obviously figures like these change rapidly but they do give an indication of the wider economic climate, which is an important factor when thinking about debt. For example, for around 12 years, starting in the early 1990s, the economy has seen a heady mixture of increasing house prices, low unemployment and low inflation.

All of these factors mean that there were more people in work with a large asset that was increasing in value each year. At the same time the cost of many products and services, for example cars, holidays, was relatively low. As a consequence, people felt very confident about borrowing money as they were confident about their jobs and had equity in their houses. The banks and other financial institutions felt similarly confident and were happy to lend out money.

From 2008 onwards the picture changed significantly as it became apparent that many people who borrowed money were not in a position to pay it back. At the same time, there were fears over employment, which led to a lack of confidence among consumers and the banks. What started as a 'credit crunch' led on to a recession. The result of this is that people began to lose their jobs and were unable to pay their debts. At the same time it became much harder to borrow money.

The net result of this is that the tail end of 2008 and most of 2009 saw an increasing number of people in debt crisis, as well as a large number of people unable to get the credit they needed, particularly people wanting to buy houses and people running businesses.

It is very difficult for us as consumers to predict what might happen in the future. It is apparent that most of the country's financial 'experts' didn't see the credit crunch coming so what chance do we have? What we can do, however, is ensure that our personal financial plans, particularly in relation to taking on debts, do take account of the worst case scenario.

Debt management

The term 'debt management' is being used in the broadest sense here so it is not just about managing debts once they start to become a problem. Instead it is about the whole process of thinking about what debts you may or may not take on and looking at the effect this will have on your monthly budgeting. It is also about thinking ahead to consider the longer term implications of the debt.

Much of this is a simple case of budgeting as we saw in Chapter 1. It is possible to know exactly how much a debt will cost by looking at the APR. For example, with a loan, the provider will provide you with an exact monthly repayment amount. You can also use one of the online loan calculators, for example: www.moneymadeclear.fsa.gov.uk/tools.aspx?Tool=loan_calculator.

A typical loan illustration looks like this:

Amount of loan: £10,000
APR: 8.9%
Repayment period: 48 months
Monthly payment: £248.38
Total repayable: £11,922.04
Total paid for credit: £1,922.04

There are a number of questions you might ask yourself before taking this on:

What am I using the money for and do I really need to borrow it?

If you are borrowing money to improve your house or start a business it may well be that you expect that the £10,000 spent will actually lead to you being better off. You may be spending the money on a wedding, dream holiday or car, in which case you may feel that you really do need the money straight away. In other circumstances you may think twice about borrowing the money at all.

Can I afford this now and every month for the next four years?

You may be confident that you can afford the repayments now but you are committing to four years of monthly payments. What if your circumstances change? What if you lose your job?

Is the APR fixed or variable?

With a fixed APR you can be confident that the monthly repayment will not change and this makes it easier for budgeting purposes. You might expect your salary to increase over the next four years in which case the repayment becomes a smaller part of your outgoings. However, if the APR is variable then the repayments could go up or down significantly. If they go up, can you still afford the repayments?

What other debts do I have?

Related to the point above, you might be able to afford all your debts now, but if the rates go up, they will go up on all of your borrowing.

What if I lose my job?

Do you have payment protection insurance? Would it force you into selling your house? How much leeway have you got?

What happens if I can't pay the monthly amounts?

This could vary depending on what type of loan you have and what it's for. The scariest possibility is that you lose your house if you have debts secured against it. More on this aspect later.

Am I prepared to pay £1,922.04 for the benefit of having it now?

This is very much a personal decision and will depend to an extent on what the money is for. If it's for a car you may feel that it is worth paying because you really need the car now, not least to get to work. If it's for a holiday you might decide to spend a bit longer saving up.

Can I get a lower APR elsewhere?

If you are convinced that you need to borrow the money then you need to shop around now and look to switch if a significantly better offer becomes available at a later stage.

If you want to stay on top of your debts it is important to have a plan. The first part of that plan is to ensure that you need to borrow the money and that you are fully aware of the cost of credit both now and for the entire period that the money is owed.

The second stage is to use your budget plan to see what effect this has on your monthly outgoings and to make sure you can afford it now and in the future. There is an element of guesswork here as you do not know what you future earnings will be. There is also an element of confidence. If you are feeling confident about your job and your work prospects then you may feel safer in taking on a debt.

The next stage is to make sure that you have the right kind of debt. In Chapter 3 we looked at the different ways of borrowing money and it is important that you match the right financial product with your needs. For example, short-term borrowing on credit cards and overdrafts has a higher APR than a loan, but might be the best option if you only need to borrow the money for a very short period of time. Conversely, if you want to borrow money to buy a car then a personal loan would probably be the best option.

The next stage is to keep on top of the debt. This means paying the monthly amount every month and avoiding the temptation to take any payment holidays that might be on offer. You may also consider repaying the debt early if your circumstances change and you find yourself better off than you expected or if you find a much better deal and choose to switch.

If you do decide to repay early, it is worth checking for additional charges. These occur because the total amount you pay is worked out by the provider assuming that the debt will run its full term. If you pay it off early the provider gets less in interest, which is why there might be early settlement charges. The law is changing on this in 2010 at which time you should only be charged up to two months' worth of interest for early settlement.

Getting out of debt

Many people decide that they want a debt-free life. This is either because they are worried about debt crisis or simply because they want to. The latter often happens to people later in life as they start to earn more and have higher levels of savings. At the same time their mortgage is taking up a smaller part of their outgoings and perhaps they have children who are now becoming independent. Even if you don't fall into this category it is possible to reduce your debts to the bare minimum. Much of this depends on your state of mind. We do live in a 'buy it now' culture and it can be hard to break this habit. You may not be able to do all of these things, but you could consider the following:

▶ *Reduce your spending: use your budget plan to make small economies across the board. These add up to large savings.*
▶ *Chop up your credit and store cards: how many things did you pay for on those cards that you wouldn't have bought if you didn't have that card handy?*
▶ *Pay off important and expensive debts first: pay your mortgage first and any other debts secured against your property. Look at the debts with the highest APR and clear these next.*
▶ *Have a* **'debt management plan'** *or DMP. This is a plan set up to pay off your non-priority creditors.*
▶ *Consolidate your debts: lump all of your borrowing together into one debt. (More on this later.)*
▶ *Pay more than the minimum amount: paying just the monthly minimum will extend the life of the debt significantly and increase the total interest payable.*
▶ *Stick to the plan: paying off regular amounts will reduce the debt quicker and you will avoid late payment charges.*
▶ *Have faith: it can take time to clear debts and this time goes slower than the time it took to spend it in the first place!*

You might also consider getting financial advice, either face-to-face or via the Internet, from one of the money charities or the Citizen's Advice Bureau (CAB), although these tend to be for people who are in crisis. You could use an IFA who will help you look at all of your spending and debt and advise on the best way to structure your debt.

There are many providers who now offer a '**debt consolidation**' service. The idea of this is that they pay off all of your debts for you and reduce the total amount you need to repay each month. You need to be very careful with these providers. On the plus side you are saved the hassle of dealing with all of the companies that you owe money to as the debt consolidations company will do it on your behalf. They will also reduce your monthly payments. On the down side, they can only decrease your monthly payments by putting the loan over a longer period. So although it appears cheaper, in the long run you will be paying much more and this is how they make their money.

Debt consolidation can save you significant amounts of money, particularly if APRs have come down since you took out the debts. The best advice is to shop around for a deal yourself. You can apply to any bank or loan company for a consolidation loan and these may offer lower APRs than the loan consolidation specialists. The trick then is to make sure that you don't borrow any more money because you find you have extra money at the end of the month.

Insight

Mr and Mrs U were not in debt crisis but were finding it increasingly difficult to service their two loans, overdraft, credit and store card debts. They owed a total of around £9,000 at APRs varying from 9% to 30%. They decided to take out one loan for £9,000 at 12.8% to repay all the debts. They took the loan out over five years. On the plus side they now had one monthly payment which was less than the total of the previous repayments. On the downside they would be paying back the money over a longer period which increases the total amount repayable.

Debt crisis

Debt crisis is when you can no longer afford to meet the minimum repayments on your debts. The impact of this is:

▶ *You can have your house repossessed if you fail to pay your mortgage or any other loan secured against your house.*
▶ *You could have possessions repossessed if you fail to keep up the payments on them.*
▶ *You can ruin your credit history making it difficult to borrow money in the future.*
▶ *You could be forced into personal bankruptcy.*
▶ *There can be a social stigma attached to debt and bankruptcy.*

So that's the worst that could happen and it is quite bad. However, the scary outcomes described above are at the very end of the line and it is not really in anyone's interest for things to get this far. For example, the building society would much rather work out repayment terms with the home owner than force them out and then have to auction off the house, getting less than the full market value.

It takes months or even years for lenders to get to the stage where they are going to court to get their money back and there is a lot that you can do before it gets to this stage if you find yourself in trouble. It is worth mentioning that people get into debt crisis for a variety of reasons and it is not simply a case of irresponsible borrowing. Personal circumstances such as redundancy, illness, death in the family or divorce all have a massive impact on the family finances. It can often be the perceived social stigma of being in debt that compounds the problem. Many people in debt tend to ignore it for as long as possible hoping it will sort itself out. Early action can significantly improve the outcome.

Insight

Mr and Mrs Y got into trouble with their debts when Mr Y was made redundant. They were unable to keep up all their
(Contd)

repayments in full. They contacted all of their creditors immediately and negotiated short-term reductions in their repayments. They prioritized the mortgage and although only paying 75% of what they normally paid the building society were satisfied with this, which held off any threat of repossession.

You may feel you are in debt crisis or approaching it if:

▶ *You can't make the minimum repayments on your credit cards.*
▶ *You are skipping monthly payments on loans or your mortgage.*
▶ *You are borrowing money, for example on overdraft or on your credit card, just to live.*
▶ *The amount you owe goes up every month and the situation shows no sign of improvement.*

It can take months or years to get into debt crisis and it is a bit of a self-fulfilling cycle. You borrow money to live because you have debts, which in turn increases the debt so you need to borrow even more to live. So how do you escape the spiral?

The first step is to look at your income and see if there is any way of increasing it. There may be simple ways of increasing your income by taking on a part-time job. You may be able to make money from your assets by selling them or down-grading them. It may be that your circumstances have changed and that you are entitled to state benefits, which previously you were not, particularly if there has been redundancy, illness or death in the family.

The second step is to look at the debts and start on what could be a long and slow process of paying them off. In addition to the general advice given in the previous section on paying off debts, if you are in debt crisis you should:

▶ *Contact all of the companies that you owe money to and inform them that you are having difficulties repaying the debt. You need to engage in a dialogue with the companies.*

Think about it from their point of view. If someone owed you money, you would want to know why it wasn't being paid and when you might get it back.

▶ *Ask for more favourable repayment terms. This could be: a reduction in the total amount payable; a reduction in the monthly amount; waiving of late payment charges and other penalties. You should discuss this with the company and make them an offer as to what you can afford.*

▶ *Prioritize the biggest or most important debts. If you are struggling to pay your mortgage, it is this that you should focus on as you could lose your home.*

▶ *Seek advice from a debt charity or the Citizen's Advice Bureau. In addition to the advice they give, they may be able to contact the lenders on your behalf. Contact details of the main charities are listed in the last section of this chapter.*

▶ *Consider an Individual Voluntary Arrangement (IVA) – see next section.*

Overall, the best advice is to act quickly and not to ignore debt problems. Most lenders will respond favourably if you contact them to discuss the issue.

Bankruptcy/IVA

When you get near to the end of the line with debt problems there are two options left, bankruptcy and the Individual Voluntary Arrangement (IVA). Both are explained briefly in this section, but the best advice would be to seek the advice of one of the debt charities listed in the final section of this chapter, before embarking on either course of action.

Bankruptcy is when you legally declare that you are unable to pay off your debts. You can declare yourself bankrupt or your creditors (people you owe money to) can petition the court to declare you bankrupt. It is probably the most serious financial decision you could make to declare yourself bankrupt as you are effectively admitting that you do not have control over your finances. The 'official receiver' will then go through all of your financial affairs and your assets, including your house, may be sold to pay off your debts. Any outstanding debt after this is written off. To declare yourself bankrupt you need to complete the bankruptcy application documents and apply to your local county courts who will hear your case.

Bankruptcy is usually associated with businesses although anyone, including private individuals, can declare themselves bankrupt. The process of bankruptcy is complex and can be long-winded. The disadvantages probably outweigh the advantages and as such, it is very much a last resort.

The advantages are that your debts are paid off and the remainder written off, which means that you will no longer be pursued by your creditors. The official receiver takes over your financial affairs, which essentially means you are passing all responsibility to someone else.

There are many disadvantages, the main one being that you will probably lose your home, even if you are a tenant. You will find it very difficult to borrow money again, or certainly for a number of years and may even find it difficult to get a bank account. Your affairs will be scrutinized and you will be liable for prosecution if any irregularities are found. There is also an element of stigma as the local press will probably publish your name in the court reports.

If your financial affairs are at this stage, a preferable option would be the **Individual Voluntary Arrangement** or IVA. An IVA is an agreement between you and your creditors to pay off a percentage of your debts over a five-year period. Any outstanding amounts after that are typically written off. These are set up and overseen by insolvency practitioners and are legally binding agreements. Typically you can apply for an IVA if you are employed, and owe more than £15,000 to three or more creditors.

The advantages of the IVA are that you will have more control over the proceedings, even negotiating which of your assets get sold. You are more likely to be able to stay in your own home with an IVA. There is less stigma than declaring yourself bankrupt and you can continue in your normal line of work.

However, your **creditor** must agree to the arrangement and you are legally bound to meet the repayments or you will end up being declared bankrupt. Your credit rating will be affected but not as adversely as if you were bankrupt.

Sources of help and advice – charities and other organizations

Debt is an increasing problem in the UK. Recent figures from money charity Credit Action (www.creditaction.org.uk) taken in June 2009:

- *Average household debt for those households with some form of unsecured loan is £21,570 excluding mortgages.*
- *Average borrowing per person in the UK on credit cards, loans etc is £4,850.*
- *331 people per day will go into bankruptcy.*
- *The Citizens' Advice Bureau will deal with 7,241 new queries every day.*

Insight

As a word of caution here, there are lots of organizations that claim they will help you with your debt problems. Many of these are money lending organizations whose main interest is a commercial one. Their aim is for you to consolidate all of your borrowing by taking out a loan through them. Typically these loans are over longer periods than your existing borrower and therefore appear cheaper.

There are a number of national charities who operate help lines and websites offering advice. These are listed in the table on the following page.

Charity	Website/Phone	Summary
Citizens' Advice Bureau (CAB)	www.citizensadvice.org.uk	Provide legal and financial advice including face-to-face meetings in centres located throughout the UK.
Consumer Credit Counselling Service (CCCS)	www.cccs.co.uk	Provide online debt counselling and debt management plans along with online information.
National Debt Line	www.nationaldebtline.co.uk: tel. 0808 808 4000	Provide a national telephone hotline to help people with debt problems.
Credit Action	www.creditaction.org.uk	An educational charity providing various resources via their website including links to other organizations.
The Financial Services Authority (FSA)	www.moneymadeclear.fsa.gov.uk	The government appointed regulator of the financial services industry also offer advice and resources through their website.
Cash Questions	www.cashquestions.com	A website sponsored by various financial services businesses offering independent answers to specific financial questions.

TEN IMPORTANT THINGS TO REMEMBER

1 *Most households experience debt of some kind and not all debt is a bad thing.*

2 *Debt is a major part of modern life and can have negative effects on individuals and the economy as a whole.*

3 *Debt management is about keeping on top of your debts.*

4 *Debt crisis is when you can no longer afford to pay off your debts.*

5 *All decisions about taking on extra debt should be analysed carefully in relation to your personal financial circumstances.*

6 *All decisions about debt should be considered in light of what might happen in the future and the worst case scenario.*

7 *Debt crisis can lead to the loss of your home or other assets.*

8 *You should not ignore debt problems but act quickly by contacting your creditors.*

9 *You can get an IVA or declare yourself bankrupt as the last resort.*

10 *There are several sources of free, impartial help and advice on debt problems.*

11

Further information

In this chapter you will learn:
- **where to get further information, help and advice on everything in this book**
- **what general finance websites are available**
- **what websites you can access for financial news, help and advice**
- **where to find information on specific financial topics**
- **what comparison websites are available**

Introduction

This chapter summarizes all of the websites referenced and includes additional websites for those wishing to extend their reading. Financial information is changing all the time and your decisions should always be based on the latest figures.

It is worth pointing out that the website addresses were accurate at the time of publication, but they do come and go. Furthermore, we are not recommending these websites as such, and you should exercise your own judgement before acting on any advice that they may give. We have indicated who is responsible for each website listed so you will know whether it is owned by the government, a charity or not-for-profit organization, a business, the press or a private individual.

General websites

Address	Owner	Summary
www.bankofengland.co.uk	Bank of England	Policies and statistics on the economy and financial markets.
www.statistics.gov.uk	Office of National Statistics	Statistics on all aspects of the economy and spending.
www.hm-treasury.gov.uk	The Treasury	All aspects of economic policy and government policy.
www.berr.gov.uk	The Department for Business, Innovation and Skills	Employment and business information.
www.direct.gov.uk	UK government	A range of advice and information with particular emphasis on tax and benefits.

News, help and advice websites

Address	Owner	Summary
www.moneymadeclear.fsa.gov.uk	Financial Services Authority	Consumer advice on all aspects of financial services.
www.fsa.gov.uk	Financial Services Authority	Main site of the financial services regulator.
www.oft.gov.uk	Office of Fair Trading	Advice for consumers of a range of products and services. Information on scams.
www.financial-ombudsman.org.uk	Independent body set up by parliament.	Intervene in complaints between consumers and financial services organizations.
www.moneysavingexpert.com	Money journalist Martin Lewis	General advice and money saving tips.
www.thisismoney.co.uk	Daily Mail	Online newspaper covering all aspects of money and personal finance.
www.helptheaged.org.uk	UK charity	Specific advice on money issues for older people.

(Contd)

Address	Owner	Summary
www.consumerdirect.gov.uk	UK government	Advice for consumers on a range of products and services.
www.moneyadvicetrust.org	UK charity	Independent money and debt advice.
www.fool.co.uk	Private business	Online journal on all aspects of money and personal finance.
www.citizensadvice.org.uk	UK charity	Advice on a range of consumer issues and money problems.
www.cccs.co.uk	Not-for-profit organization	Advice and help on debt.
www.nationaldebtline.co.uk	Money Advice Trust	Advice on debt.
www.creditaction.org.uk	UK charity	Advice and facts on debt.
www.cashquestions.com	Operated by journalists and sponsored by financial services businesses.	Allows you to ask an expert on any aspect of money and personal finance.

Subject-specific websites

Address	Owner	Summary
www.childtrustfund.gov.uk	UK government	Information on Child Trust Funds.
www.payingforchildcare.org.uk	UK charity (The Day Care Trust)	Information on childcare costs and assistance.
www.direct.gov.uk/en/Parents/Childcare	UK government	Information and assistance on cost of childcare.
www.ofsted.gov	Government department	Information on performance of schools.
www.isc.co.uk	Independent Schools Council	Information on private schools.
www.cafonline.org	Christian Aid Foundation Charity	Information on bursaries and scholarships available for private schooling.
http://ema.direct.gov.uk	UK government	Information on educational maintenance allowance for 16–19-year-olds continuing in education.

(Contd)

Address	Owner	Summary
http://myplatform2.com	Department for International Development	Advice on funded gap years.
http://www.direct.gov.uk/ en/EducationAndLearning/ UniversityAndHigherEducation/ StudentFinance/index.htm	UK government	Student loans and grants.
www.fscs.org.uk	Independent body set up under the Financial Services and Markets Act 2000	Information on the financial services compensation scheme for authorized organizations.
www.dmo.gov.uk	UK government	Department that sells UK gilts and bonds.
www.nsandi.com	An agency of the Chancellor of the Exchequer	Offer a range of savings and investment products backed by HM Treasury.
www.whatinvestment.co.uk	Independently owned magazine.	Specializes in investments.
www.ftse.com	Independently owned by the *Financial Times* and The Stock Exchange	Information on publicly listed UK businesses including share prices.
www.thepensionservice.gov.uk	UK government	Information and advice on state pensions.

Address	Owner	Summary
www.fsa.gov.uk/tables	Financial Services Authority	Comparison tables of pension providers.
www.cml.org.uk	Council for mortgage lenders	General information on the pensions market.
www.homeinformationpacks.gov.uk	UK government	Information on home information packs for house buyers and sellers.
http://mortgagehelp.direct.gov.uk/index.html	UK government	Advice on the mortgage rescue scheme.
www.ccwater.org.uk	Water consumer council	Includes water usage calculator.
www.getsafeonline.org	Office of Fair Trading	Information on the latest Internet scams.
www.bankingcode.org.uk	Banking Code Standards Board	Information on the way in which banks should deal with customers.
http://www.direct.gov.uk/en/MoneyTaxAndBenefits/Taxes/BeginnersGuideToTax/IncomeTax/Taxallowancesandreliefs/index.htm	UK government	Guidance on tax and National Insurance.

(Contd)

Address	Owner	Summary
http://www.hmrc.gov.uk/sa/introduction.htm	UK government	Help on self-assessment
http://www.voa.gov.uk/council_tax/index.htm	UK government	Explanation of valuation of households for council tax.
http://www.direct.gov.uk/en/MoneyTaxAndBenefits/Taxes/InheritanceTaxEstatesAndTrusts/DG_4016736	UK government	Guidance on inheritance tax.
http://ukonline.direct.gov.uk/en/MoneyTaxAndBenefits/BenefitsTaxCreditsAndOtherSupport/BeginnersGuideToBenefits/index.htm	UK government	Guidance on state benefits.
www.dwp.gov.uk	UK government	Issues relating to employment including payment of some benefits.
http://www.jobcentreplus.gov.uk/JCP/index.html	UK government	Issues relating to employment and unemployment including the payment of some benefits.
http://campaigns.dwp.gov.uk/campaigns/benefit-thieves	UK government	To report benefits cheats.

Address	Owner	Summary
www.tradingstandards.gov.uk	Trading Standards	Information and advice on mis-selling or rogue traders.
www.ofwat.gov.uk	UK regulatory body	Advice on issues relating to your water supply.
www.ofgem.gov.uk	UK regulatory body	Advice on issues relating to your gas and electricity supply.
www.ofcom.org.uk	UK regulatory body	Advice on issues relating to your telecoms supply.
www.experian.com	Credit referencing agency	Check your credit rating.
www.equifax.co.uk	Credit referencing agency	Check your credit rating.
www.callcredit.co.uk	Credit referencing agency	Check your credit rating.
www.unbiased.co.uk	Private business	Information on independent financial advisers (IFAs) including registers of registered IFAs in your area.
http://www.consumerdirect.gov.uk/ watch_out/Commonscams/ID_theft	UK government	Information and advice on common scams.
http://www.identitytheft.org.uk	UK government and other agencies	Advice and guidance on identity theft and how to avoid it.

Comparison and switching websites

www.moneysupermarket.com
www.confused.com
www.comparethemarket.com
www.gocompare.com
www.switchwithwhich.co.uk
www.uswitch.co.uk

Glossary

accident, sickness and redundancy insurance Insurance that covers you if you are unable to work due to accident, sickness or redundancy.

account A financial arrangement between you and a financial services institution.

account charges The amount you pay for services provided on any account you have with a financial services institution.

account number Usually an eight-digit number that uniquely identifies your account.

allowances In relation to income tax, these reduce the amount of tax you have to pay.

Annual Equivalent Rate (AER) The amount of interest you earn from your savings. Shown as a percentage over the year.

Annual Percentage Rate (APR) The amount on interest you pay on borrowed money. Shown as a percentage over the year.

annuity A product that you buy in retirement that guarantees you an annual income.

arrangement fee The amount a financial services provider will charge you when you buy certain financial products e.g. a mortgage.

asset Anything that you own.

ATM Auto-teller machine or cash point machine.

ATM card Card used in an ATM or cash point machine.

authorized overdraft An arrangement made with the bank to spend more money than you have via your current account.

bank balance The amount of money you have in a bank account.

bank statement A document that shows all the money going in and out of your bank account and the amount you have left.

Banking Code Standards Board A committee with representatives from the banks who set the standards by which banks should treat their customer.

bankruptcy The financial status of someone who cannot pay their debts and goes to court to declare this.

Base Rate The interest rate set by the Bank of England, which is how much they charge UK banks when they lend them money.

benefits See state benefits.

bonds A financial product that you buy from a government or an organization which then pays interest.

budgeting The process of keeping track of all of your income and expenses.

budget plan A document that shows all your income and expenses and what you have left.

buildings insurance Insurance that pays for repairs or rebuilding if your house is damaged or destroyed.

bursary A payment made to a student if they enrol on a particular course.

Capital Gains Tax (CGT) A tax payable when you sell certain assets and make a profit from the sale, e.g. a second home.

cash flow The amount of money that you have available in cash right now.

cash ISA A tax-free individual savings account.

Child Trust Fund (CTF) A payment made by the government to the parents of all children when they are born and again when they are aged seven.

children's bond A savings product you can buy that is specifically designed for your child. Usually tax free.

cleared item Any payment made into your account which you can now spend, e.g. a cheque or transfer.

clearing The process banks use of ensuring that money has passed from one bank account to another.

company pension A pension scheme where the company make contributions as well as the individual.

complaints procedure The stated policy of a financial services institution as to how they will deal with any customer complaints.

comprehensive insurance Car insurance that covers you even if the accident is your fault.

consolidation loan A loan which is taken out to pay off other loans or debts.

Consumer Credit Act A law which gives consumers certain protection and rights when buying financial products and services.

consumer rights Legal rights that we have whenever we buy products and services.

contents insurance Insurance that covers the contents of your home.

contingency The process of allowing a bit extra in case of emergencies – usually in relation to budgeting.

council tax A tax payable by every household to the local council to pay for local services, e.g. schools and police.

credit Any form of lending.

credit card Plastic card that can be used to pay for purchases where the money is not actually in the bank. The customer pays it off later.

credit crunch An economic situation where individuals and businesses find it difficult to borrow money because no one wants to lend it.

credit history Your personal record of when you have borrowed money and whether you paid it back or not.

credit rating Your personal rating in terms of suitability to borrow money.

credit referencing The process of checking that you are a suitable and reliable person to lend money to.

credit scoring The system that the banks use to assess whether you are credit-worthy or not.

creditor Anyone you owe money to.

critical illness cover Insurance designed to pay out if you are unable to work due to a serious or life-threatening illness.

current account An account provided by a bank that you use for everyday transactions.

debit card Plastic card that can be used to pay for purchases but the funds must be available at the time you use the card.

debt Anything you owe.

debt consolidation Putting all of your debts into one place in order to pay them off.

debt crisis When you can no longer afford the minimum repayments on your borrowing.

debt management The process of managing the payments on all the money you owe.

debt management plan A specific plan usually set up with a debt counselling service to clear your debts – usually when you are in debt crisis.

debtor Anyone who owes you money.

decreasing insurance policy In relation to life insurance, the amount payable reduces as the years pass.

deposit An amount paid to secure the purchase of something – typically a house.

direct debit An automated payment from your bank account, e.g. to pay the gas bill.

discounted mortgage A mortgage with a low interest rate in the first year or two. Typically offered to first-time buyers.

early-repayment penalties The amount that a financial services provider will charge you if you pay off any borrowing before the stated time.

economy The general term to describe all of the business and financial activity taking place in the country.

Educational Maintenance Allowance (EMA) A payment made to some 16–19-year-olds if they stay on in full-time education.

endowment/endowment policy An insurance policy that pays out a set amount after a certain number of years and includes life cover if you die before it matures.

equity A general term for money that you have available to you even if it is tied up in an asset.

ethical investment Any investment where your money will not end up in companies that deal in unethical businesses, e.g. the arms trade.

Excel A computer program for manipulating figures. Particularly useful for all types of financial calculations, e.g. a budget.

excess The amount payable by you when you make a claim on your insurance.

expenses In budgeting, these are all of your outgoings, i.e. the money you spend.

Family Income Benefit A type of life insurance policy that pays out a regular annual sum (rather than a lump sum) in the event of someone's death.

finance deal Any arrangement where you buy products on credit.

Financial Ombudsman Service A government-backed scheme to mediate in disputes between customers and financial services providers.

Financial Services Authority (FSA) The government backed agency who regulate the banking and financial sectors in the UK.

Financial Services Compensation Scheme (FSCA) A government-backed scheme that guarantees your savings up to a value of £50,000 in any one institution.

fixed rate account A savings account that offers a set AER over a fixed period, usually around a year. You cannot get access to your money in this time without heavy penalties.

fixed-rate mortgage A mortgage where the interest rate is fixed for a set number of years.

fixed rates Indicates that interest rates will not change for a set number of years, e.g. on a loan.

fixed savings bonds A savings product that pays you a fixed rate of interest for a set number of years.

flexible mortgage A mortgage where the customer can vary the monthly repayments over time.

gap year A year off usually between school and university where young people work or travel.

gilts Government bonds.

grant A payment made to individuals (under certain circumstances) to assist them to do something, e.g. student grants for those on low income.

Gross A general term for a total amount prior to tax being deducted, e.g. Gross income.

health insurance A type of insurance policy that pays out for private medical treatment.

health plans A type of insurance that entitles you to set amounts of money for particular treatments, e.g. dental care.

Home Information Pack (HIP) Information that a house seller must pass on to potential buyers.

identity theft When a criminal acquires personal details about you that allows them to pretend to be you – usually to commit a fraud.

income Any money that you have coming in, e.g. from your job, or interest on savings.

income bonds A type of bond that offers a regular interest payment.

income tax Payments made directly out of your wages to the government to pay for public services.

Independent Financial Adviser (IFA) An individual qualified to advise you when you are buying financial products and services.

index-linked Where the amount payable from a financial product is linked to some external measure, e.g. the cost of living.

index-linked bonds A bond that is linked to the cost of living so that the amount of interest goes up and down accordingly.

Individual Savings Account (ISA) A tax free savings account.

Individual Voluntary Arrangement (IVA) An arrangement between an individual and their creditors to pay off a reduced amount where the individual is in debt crisis.

inflation The amount by which goods and services go up each year in the UK economy as a whole.

Inheritance Tax (IHT) A tax payable on any assets inherited.

instalment A part payment, usually as part of a series of payments.

instant access account A savings account where you get access to you money instantly if you need it.

insurance The payment of a premium to protect yourself against future risks.

interest rate The percentage that you pay when you borrow money or receive when you save money.

interest-only mortgage A mortgage where you only pay off the interest leaving the lump sum to pay at the end.

Investment Trust A scheme offered by a financial services provider where they will invest your money in a range of things.

investments A general term for any financial product where you put your money in with the expectation of getting more out.

level term insurance A type of life insurance policy that guarantees to pay out a fixed amount on the event of the death of the policy holder.

life insurance A type of insurance that pays out if the policy holder dies. Some policies also cover terminal illnesses.

loan Any form of borrowing where a set amount is borrowed and repaid monthly.

loan to value (LTV) The ratio that lenders use when deciding how much mortgage to give you, e.g. 80% LTV means that they will lend you 80% of the value of the house.

loyalty card Used by retailers, these offer points equivalent to discounts, every time you buy something and show the card.

lump sum When an amount is paid all in one go rather than in instalments.

maintenance grant Available to students whose household income is below a certain amount. To be used for living costs while studying. Does not have to be paid back.

maintenance loan Available to students to be used for living costs while studying. Has to be paid back when the student gets a job that pays above a set income level.

management fee The amount a financial services provider will charge you for the ongoing management of a product or service, e.g. a pension.

minimum wage The hourly rate set by government which all workers must be paid.

mortgage A long-term loan to buy property or land.

multiple In mortgage terms, this is the total amount the lender will lend you based on your salary, e.g. a multiple of three times your annual salary.

National Insurance (NI) A government tax used to pay for state benefits including the state pension.

net A general term to indicate the amount after tax e.g. net income.

no-claims bonus In car insurance this is the discount that you will get based on the number of years that you have not claimed on your policy.

no-claims discount (NCD) In car insurance this is the discount that you will get based on the number of years that you have not claimed on your policy.

notice account A savings account where you let the bank know in advance that you want to withdraw all or part of your money. The notice period could be anything from one month upwards.

Office of Fair Trading (OFT) The government agency responsible for the way that businesses in general deal with the public.

offset mortgage A type of mortgage where you pay less interest if you forgo interest payable on your savings.

online banking Managing your bank account via the Internet.

overdraft A facility provided by your bank where you spend more money than you have in your current account.

overdraft charges The amount the bank will charge you for your overdraft facility.

overdraft limit The amount the bank will let you go overdrawn each month.

overdrawn When the balance on your bank account is a minus figure.

Pay As You Earn (PAYE) Income tax where the amount you pay is based on the amount you earn.

Payment Protection Insurance (PPI) A type of insurance policy that will pay off any borrowing in the event that you are unable to work.

pension A savings scheme that pays out when you stop working.

personal allowance The amount you are allowed to earn before you start paying tax.

personal loan A loan that is offered based on your personal circumstances and your ability to pay it back.

personal pension A type of pension where you choose the provider; you choose from a range of funds with different levels of risk attached and set up a monthly direct debit. When the fund is big enough you cash it in.

pet insurance A type of insurance that pays out if you need medical treatment for your pet or if it is lost.

phishing The criminal act of trying to get you to part with your bank details via emails that appear to be from your bank.

PIN A four-digit code needed to use your credit or debit card or an ATM.

planned overdraft An arrangement with the bank to spend more money than you have in your current account.

premium A payment for insurance.

premium current bank account A bank account that offers extra services but comes with a monthly fee.

Premium Bonds A government backed savings product where each bond is entered into a monthly prize draw.

price comparison website A website that compares the costs of various financial products and services and ranks them in price order.

private pension A pension scheme where you pay in as an individual over a number of years.

rainy day money Spare money that you keep just in case something unexpected happens, e.g. redundancy.

recession An economic situation where there is reduced activity and high unemployment.

regulation Laws instigated by the courts or the government.

repayment mortgage A type of mortgage where the total sum borrowed and total interest are added together and the monthly repayment is calculated to cover both by the end of the mortgage period.

savings Putting money away for use later on.

savings account Any facility that allows you to put your money into it for access at a later stage.

scam Any con or fiddle where a criminal tries to trick us into giving them either money or information that they can use for identity theft.

scholarship Money offered to individual students to attend a particular school or university. Usually for specific reasons.

secured loan Any loan where your house is used as collateral. This means if you don't repay the loan your house could be sold to recover the money.

self-assessment A form sent by the tax office where you have to declare your income for income tax reasons.

self-invested pension plan (SIPP) A type of pension where the individual takes an active role in deciding where the money being saved will be invested.

share trading The process of buying and selling shares in businesses listed on the stock market.

shares Part ownership of a business.

sort code A six-digit number that identifies your bank and branch.

spending Any outgoings. Usually used in budgeting terms to indicate all the money that you spend each month.

spreadsheet A computer program for manipulating figures. Particularly useful for all types of financial calculations e.g. a budget.

stakeholder pension Very similar to a personal pension where the individual makes payments into their own pension pot.

stamp duty A tax payable when you buy a house.

standing order A type of payment that can be made between your bank and another organization's bank, e.g. to pay your council tax.

state benefits Money paid to individuals by the government in particular circumstances, e.g. unemployed, disabled, elderly people.

state pension Money paid by the state to older people as income.

stocks and shares ISA A tax free savings account where the money you save is invested in the stock market.

store card Similar to a credit card but only usable in one store or chain of stores.

student fees The amount payable to students each year that is then paid to the university to pay for tuition.

student grant An amount payable to students below a certain income. Does not have to paid back.

student loan An amount payable to students. Has to be paid back when the student is working.

survey Required by the bank or building society when you buy a house.

switching The process of swapping from one financial services or utilities provider to another.

tax code Sent by the tax office each year, this indicates how much you can earn before you have to pay tax.

tax return A form sent by the tax office where you have to account for all of your income for income tax purposes.

telephone banking The process of banking via a call-centre.

third-party insurance Car insurance that covers the other person if you are in an accident but does not cover you if it is your fault.

third-party, fire and theft insurance As third-party but also pays out if your car is damaged or destroyed by fire or stolen.

tracker mortgage A type of mortgage where the interest rate is tied in with the Bank of England Base Rate.

Trading Standards Agency A government backed agency that enforces laws relating to the way that businesses deal with their customers.

transaction In banking terms this relates to any activity where money changes hands, e.g. a transfer.

transaction fee The amount that a financial services provider will charge you for carrying out a particular service.

travel insurance A type of insurance that pays out if you need to get home due to accident or illness or if you lose your luggage while on holiday.

typical APR This is the amount that lenders must quote when lending money to indicate the APR that most people will get.

unauthorized overdraft When you spend more than you have in your current account and do not inform the bank.

uncleared item A payment or receipt that has not gone through the banking system yet but is pending, e.g. a cheque.

unemployment In economic terms this refers to the total number of people who are out of work.

unit and investment trust A type of investment where your money is pooled with other investors.

unplanned overdraft When you spend more than you have in your current account and do not inform the bank.

unsecured personal loan A loan that is offered based on your personal circumstances and your ability to pay it back.

utilities Generic term for gas, electricity, water and telecoms.

Value Added Tax (VAT) A tax payable on most products we buy.

watchdog An agency set up by the government to monitor particular industries – usually ones that used to be state controlled, e.g. gas and electricity.

Index